reading aids series

# literacy for america's spanish speaking children

Eleanor Wall Thonis
Marysville Reading-Learning Center
Olivehurst, California

Review Editor     Alfonso R. Ramirez

an  service bulletin

international reading association • newark delaware 19711

# INTERNATIONAL READING ASSOCIATION

## OFFICERS
## 1976-1977

*President*   Walter H. MacGinitie, Teachers College, Columbia University, New York, New York

*Vice-President*   William Eller, State University of New York at Buffalo, Amherst, New York

*Vice-President Elect*   Dorothy S. Strickland, Kean College of New Jersey, Union, New Jersey

*Past President*   Thomas C. Barrett, University of Wisconsin, Madison, Wisconsin

*Executive Director*   Ralph C. Staiger, International Reading Association, Newark, Delaware

## DIRECTORS

*Term expiring Spring 1977*

Roger Farr, Indiana University, Bloomington, Indiana
Grayce A. Ransom, University of Southern California, Los Angeles, California
Harry W. Sartain, University of Pittsburgh, Pittsburgh, Pennsylvania

*Term expiring 1978*

Roselmina Indrisano, Boston University, Boston, Massachusetts
Ethna R. Reid, Exemplary Center for Reading Instruction, Salt Lake City, Utah
Robert B. Ruddell, University of California, Berkeley, California

*Term expiring Spring 1979*

Lou E. Burmeister, University of Texas, El Paso, Texas
Jack Cassidy, Newark School District, Newark, Delaware
Kenneth S. Goodman, University of Arizona, Tucson, Arizona

Copyright 1976 by the
International Reading Association, Inc.

**Library of Congress Cataloging in Publication Data**
Thonis, Eleanor.
   Literacy for America's Spanish speaking children.

   (Reading aids series) (An IRA service bulletin)
   Bibliography: p.
   1. Education, Bilingual—United States.   2. Reading—Study and teaching.   3. Spanish language—Study and teaching.   I. Title.
LC3731.T53         371.9'7'68073         76-16174
ISBN 0-87207-221-5

## CONTENTS

Foreword  *v*

Introduction  *vii*

*1* The Spanish Speaking Child
   A Point of View  *1*
   The Strengths of the Spanish Speaking Child  *4*
   The Demands of the School  *4*
   An Appropriate Reading Program  *5*
   The Young Child Who Speaks Spanish  *6*
   The Child Who Speaks Spanish and English  *7*
   The Spanish Speaking Literate Child  *8*
   The Functionally Illiterate Child  *10*
   The Dominant Language  *11*
      The Marysville Test of Language Dominance  *11*
      Test of Listening Comprehension  *13*
      Test of Speaking  *13*
      Test of Reading  *14*
      Test of Writing  *14*
      Cultural Variables  *15*
      Prueba de Comprensión Auditiva  *16*
      Prueba de Hablar  *16*
      Prueba de Lectura  *17*
      Prueba de Escribir  *17*
      Variaciones Culturales  *18*
      Oral Language Assessment for Diagnosis and Planning  *20*
      Evaluación de Lenguaje Oral para Diagnosticar y Planear  *21*

*23* Reading Program Alternatives for the Spanish Speaking Child
   Literacy in a Second Language  *23*
   Traditional Reading Approaches in English  *24*
   Literacy in the Native Language  *27*
   Traditional Reading Approaches in Spanish  *28*
   Selecting Materials  *33*
      Criteria for Selecting Materials  *33*
   Social-Cultural Content  *35*

*36* The Developmental Nature of Literacy
   Literacy Is a Task for Middle Childhood  *36*
   Literacy Has a Speech-Print Relationship  *40*
   Literacy Requires Sensorimotor Integration  *41*

    Literacy Demands Visual and Auditory Memory   *42*
    Literacy Is Thought   *44*
    Organizing the Reading Program   *44*
    Literacy Is Measurable   *45*
    Standardized Tests of Reading: A Warning   *46*
    Theoretical Considerations   *47*
    Practical Implications   *49*
    An Index of Reading Difficulty   *52*
        Buchanan and Rodriguez-Bou Word List   *55*
    Literacy and Two Language Systems   *60*
    Unresolved Issues   *62*

*64*   Literacy Puts It All Together
    The Child   *64*
    The Alternative Selected   *64*
    The Program   *65*
    References   *67*
    Additional Suggested Readings   *68*

## FOREWORD

Until the advent of bilingual education, the teaching of reading in the United States was presumed to be in English only. For years, United States teachers have led students speaking other languages through courses in reading designed for monolingual English speakers, thereby compounding the difficulties that face most beginning readers.

Now that alternatives are available, we find that native English orientation to literacy is inadequate for dealing with reading programs for speakers of other languages. For this reason, the Board of Directors of IRA appointed a committee to prepare a manuscript concerning the teaching of reading to pupils whose mother tongue is Spanish—the largest non-English language group in United States schools.

Although the charge for preparing the manuscript was given to a committee of twelve, the writing was done entirely by one of its members. The remaining committee members helped with the outline and with suggestions after the first draft; but the sole author of this valuable addition to the literature on reading instruction is Eleanor Thonis, Director of the Marysville Reading Learning Center in Olivehurst, California. Her extensive background in both English and Spanish reading gives this volume the authenticity few of us could have provided. We are indebted to her for the time and effort she donated to this project.

A. R. Ramirez, *Chairperson*
IRA Committee on Teaching Reading to Spanish Speaking Students

*Committee Members:* Tracy Tyler, Jr., Ana S. Covarrubias, Donald E. Critchlow, Jim E. Esquibel, Ramiro Garcia, Charles H. Herbert, Alonso M. Perales, Anthony R. Sancho, Maria Strandburg, Eleanor Thonis, and Robert T. Williams.

The International Reading Association attempts, through its publications, to provide a forum for a wide spectrum of opinion on reading. This policy permits divergent viewpoints without assuming the endorsement of the Association.

## INTRODUCTION

For over one hundred years, Spanish speaking school children in the United States have been placed in English reading programs. Teachers, administrators, and parents have traditionally felt that the sooner these pupils could be immersed in the English writing system, the better their reading achievement would be. Despite many attempts to modify reading programs and to make them more reasonable for pupils whose native language is Spanish, these children have continued to experience a high degree of school failure. For example, at the fourth grade level an estimated 51 percent of the Mexican-American pupils in schools of the Southwest are reading significantly below grade level. Approximately 16 percent of the first grade Spanish speaking children repeat the first grade. The repetition of grades by Spanish speaking pupils has not contributed much to better school performance and generally has not increased their reading achievement but rather has predisposed the pupils to a higher dropout rate.* Their subsequent ability to compete in the English speaking employment market has been limited by their school failure and by their inadequate control of English print.

At a time in the history of public education when the schools are expected to bring renewed concern and vigorous action in providing for the many individual differences found among pupils of all ethnic backgrounds, the learning problems of Spanish speaking children appear high on the list of priorities. Classes in remedial reading, programs of compensatory education, and lessons in English as-a-Second Language have proliferated in schools of the Southwest and in other areas of the country where Spanish speaking children are enrolled. In many instances, such programs have been very successful in helping children cope better with the rigors of a curriculum carried for them in the weaker language—English. For some of the Spanish speaking pupils, however, such intervention has been too little or too late to make a significant difference in their school achievement. Ordinarily, pupils are provided with educational activities which are specifically designed to nurture the background skills necessary for success in beginning reading. Readiness programs usually consist of lessons in concept

*The Unfinished Education, Report of the U.S. Commission on Civil Rights, Washington, D.C.

formation, auditory discrimination, visual discrimination, visual-motor control, and directionality training. Pupils who have been successful in their acquisition of these fundamental readiness skills are then placed in the developmental reading program, a continuous plan extending from the early grades through the elementary school. This program begins with the basic introductory reading skills and follows a sequence of graded stages increasing in the levels of difficulty and complexity. When pupils fail to become proficient readers and fall behind the achievement expected at their grade level, they often are assigned to programs of remedial reading. Such programs offer pupils opportunities to review earlier tasks and to explore alternative materials or methods leading to reading competence. Spanish speaking pupils who are placed in reading readiness and developmental reading programs in English are at a great disadvantage. Fragmented efforts have frequently resulted in taking pupils from reading readiness to reading remediation before they have had the opportunity to enjoy a developmental reading program appropriate for their unique language and cultural heritage.

    The purpose of this volume is threefold. First, there is a section which considers the nature of the Spanish speaking child in relation to his success in reading. The background of strengths and needs which this child brings to the classroom is discussed separately for different groups of Spanish speaking pupils: the preliterate, the literate, and the functionally illiterate pupil. Second, there is a section which explores the alternatives for helping the Spanish speaking pupil achieve literacy levels commensurate with his greatest potential. Among the alternatives presented are the various methods used in Spanish speaking countries and the traditional approaches employed in the United States. Finally, the developmental nature of reading is reviewed within the framework of first and second language literacy. This section examines the concepts of maturation and readiness, speech-print relationships, sensorimotor abilities, reading skills acquisition, and other facets of the reading program to which Spanish speaking children must respond. There are a few selected references at the end of the volume. The challenge of selecting the relevant and appropriate alternatives and of providing the best path to literacy for Spanish speaking pupils has been the overriding concern of this effort.

EWT

Chapter 1

## THE SPANISH SPEAKING CHILD

- **A Point of View**

The Spanish speaking child is first of all a child and, therefore, any consideration of his school success must first begin with the premise that his many needs, including the need for reading achievement, are exactly the same needs which stem from the universality of childhood. He needs good nutrition and good physical care; he needs affection, acceptance, and appreciation for his efforts; he needs opportunities to explore, to move, and to experience a stimulating environment. He needs a warm, supportive family and an interested, competent teacher. All children need these conditions for optimum growth and development. When considering success in reading, however, some other specific needs must be added. It is essential that all children have experiences which will nurture concept acquisition, verbal facility, and sensorimotor control. Factors of general maturation, school readiness, and interest in reading are also prerequisites of primary importance. Once these background abilities common to the needs of children in any school setting have been established, then the question of the unique needs of the Spanish speaking child and his reading achievement in schools of the United States can be examined.

It is not surprising that a reading program designed for English speaking pupils becomes a stumbling block which impedes reading achievement and creates frustration for the Spanish speaking child. For the child whose native language and cultural background are different from the traditional school curriculum, there are several conditions which contribute to failure and confusion:

1. a lack of experiences in the dominant culture from which concepts specific to the English speaking community may be acquired,
2. an inadequate oral command of the English language which is the language of the instructional program,
3. a lowered sense of self-esteem resulting from repeated feelings of inadequacy, and
4. an unrealistic curriculum which imposes reading and writing English before listening comprehension and speaking fluency have been established.

The problems of reading English which are customarily attributed to the Spanish speaking child are in reality problems of the school's own making. An inappropriate sequence and faulty pacing of skills often intensify the difficulties of the pupil who is forced to use a written symbol system for which he has no oral referent. He may be struggling with a set of sounds which he cannot perceive or discriminate. He may be expected to comprehend vocabulary and language structures which are totally alien to him. Further, he may be suffering considerable interference from his own native Spanish language—its sound, structural, lexical, and semantic systems.

There are significant differences in Spanish and English language systems which linguistic scientists have identified, analyzed, and arranged in a hierarchical order of difficulty.

Sound difficulties may occur when the English sounds do not exist in Spanish. A Spanish speaking child may not perceive these sounds and may substitute Spanish sounds for them. He may also have a problem using certain sounds he does perceive, when they exist in an unaccustomed position. Teachers have heard native Spanish speakers mispronounce English expressions like these:

1. Richard was a good *keen*.   (king)
2. I have new *choose*.   (shoes)
3. I don't *es*peak (speak) English *b*erry   (very) well.
4. I can't find the *et*ches.   (edges)
5. Little bears are called cu*p*s.   (cubs)

Structural confusions may occur when a native Spanish speaker uses variations from his own speech patterns to form words and meaningful groups of words in English. Teachers will recognize the errors which are evident in these sentences:

1. Today she *working* on the job.   (is working)
2. Both *foots* hurt.   (feet)
3. He is *more* big than his brother.   (bigger)
4. The sister *of Maria* is pretty.   (Maria's)
5. *Him* is in the house.   (He)
6. The hat *red* is at home.   (red hat)
7. I don't know *where is* the boat.   (where the boat is)
8. He saw *to* his mother.   (saw his mother)

Lexical differences may be noted particularly in the usage of various prepositions, pronouns, and verbs. Often in Spanish, *one* verb may have multiple meanings, and the context of the utterance reveals the sensible meaning. In some verbs, the preposition may be included; for example, to look for (buscar), to turn away (arrojar), to put in place (poner), to look at (mirar). When pupils attempt English expressions based upon their own Spanish vocabulary items, the result may be like these:

1. *Look* that book. (Look at)
2. *Throw* the garbage. (Throw away)
3. He is going to *put* the car. (put away)
4. *Put* the light. (put on)
5. She *handed* the report. (handed in)
6. Hang the coat *in* the wall. (on)

Other vocabulary and semantic confusions may stem from the use of words and expressions which sound like Spanish but in reality are *false cognates.* For example, *penitencia* means penance, not penitentiary; *realizar* means to accomplish an ambition, not to realize; *salvar* means to save a life, not to save money; *libreria* means bookstore, not library; *chanza* means joke, not chance.

There are many such differences in the two languages which may create problems for the child who is reading and writing in English. Since the task of the reader is to make meaningful connections between speech and print, these sound, structural, lexical, and semantic variations may interfere with or obscure meaning. Even the most skilled student who can decode the English writing system may experience difficulty in comprehending what he has decoded if interference from his native language has not been recognized by his teacher.

These examples are but a few of the potential difficulties faced by Spanish speaking pupils in reading programs designed for native speakers of English. Teachers need to be aware that the sounds and patterns of native Spanish speech have been overlearned and practiced to the point of automatic response. These well-ingrained native language habits may get in the way of the pupil's acquisition of new language responses. As a rule, his second language exposure has been somewhat limited and his opportunities for the practice which will lead him to overlearned, automatic responses in English have been considerably fewer. Further, he has learned to use his native language to organize his personal environment and to obtain meaning from his unique experiences in a Spanish speaking family. He has developed a semantic system, a storehouse of meanings encoded in Spanish, which has worked effectively within the particular cultural context in which the information has been acquired. Often, the learner becomes confused when he attempts to apply meanings internalized in one setting to other situations with different cultural and linguistic demands.

In consideration of the Spanish speaking child and his success in reading English, it is important to restate that he is primarily a child; he is unique as each child is; he shares a commonality of needs as all children do; he may have identifiable needs for broader experiences and for language development. But he cannot be viewed as a stereotype or as a child from a single mold and, therefore, a child for whom a single reading program is the answer. There is no typical Spanish speaking child in the reading programs of the United States. There are only children who need good teaching supported by relevant materials, consistent methods, and oral language opportunities as determined by an appraisal of the children themselves.

- **The Strengths of the Spanish Speaking Child**

Every teacher holds an unshakable conviction that all children have gifts. Some special strengths appear noteworthy among the Spanish speaking population of school age. The Spanish speaking child is generally a cooperative, considerate pupil who is capable of great concern and interest in helping others. He really enjoys music, art, and literature. He can put aside his own needs in deference to the needs of classmates. He responds genuinely to attention and affection and he is frequently a delight to his teacher. He is willing to try and rejoices abundantly in his successes, no matter how small. He usually possesses a strong sense of loyalty to family and friends. His shy, reserved approach, which teachers often interpret as timidity, may indeed be a display of good judgment in situations which may be new and incomprehensible. Again, it is unwise to consider that all Spanish speaking pupils of all ages exhibit all of these characteristics. Yet these traits have been noted frequently by teachers and are important because they represent attitudinal responses which can contribute positively to classroom success.

- **The Demands of the School**

For the child from a Spanish speaking family, the school may loom as a strange and threatening place inhabited by strange and threatening people. He does not understand many of the rules and regulations; he does not fully comprehend much of the teacher's instruction intended to make him feel more secure. His fears and anxieties are mild or severe depending upon the variables of his age, his previous school experiences, and his competence in English. He finds that the language system which almost from birth has helped him to control his world no longer serves him in the school. He realizes that not only does he have to acquire a new language system, he also must immediately use this new set of symbols as effective tools in his learning. He must deal with the new written language simultaneously with its oral counterpart and he must handle both with little opportunity for the repetition and the practice which is so necessary for language acquisition. As he moves directly to the symbol system of English, for which he may have little direct experience, he is bombarded with sounds which are unfamiliar to him, and he is overloaded with words and groups of words which carry little or no meaning.

In the reading program, when he attempts to recognize words by phonic or structural analysis, he cannot hear and identify many of the sounds because they have no reality in his repertoire of previously acquired language sounds. Word endings of English may not be heard because, for him, they do not exist. Comprehension of words he is able to recognize may not come easily because of the differences in his experiences, his limited vocabulary, his semantic confusion, as well as because of intermittent interference which he receives from his native language. If these problems become very severe over a prolonged period of time, the Spanish speaking child may become overwhelmed and may give up completely. His potential for success in reading English may be reduced to abject failure.

### ● An Appropriate Reading Program

Teachers have continually searched for ways to adapt materials and methods to the strengths and needs of their pupils. Recent emphasis on a diagnostic-prescriptive approach to instruction, stress on individualization, and encouragement of self-directed learning have all underscored a time-honored maxim that effective teaching begins where the child is and takes him within any given time period as far as he can comfortably go. This precept translated into the pragmatic realities of a reading program for Spanish speaking children suggests that the instructional plan cannot be designed until the teacher looks very carefully at the child for whom the plan is intended. Among the questions to be asked are:

1. How old is the child?
2. What is his present developmental level?
3. What is his past school history?
4. What is his oral native language competence?
5. To what extent has he experienced opportunities for acquiring English?
6. What exposure has he had to the Spanish writing system?
7. What English reading system has he encountered?

In addition to these concerns, there are significant social and cultural variables to be examined:

1. What language is used in his home?
2. What is the educational level of his parents?
3. Does he live in rural isolation or in an urban population center?

4. Is his present home permanent or temporary?
5. Has he had a high rate of school transfer?

For many children, it may also be necessary to investigate health factors and personal characteristics. Although some of this information may be highly general in nature, it should provide a springboard from which a more definitive assessment can be made.

It is obvious that diagnoses of potential reading strengths and weaknesses must be different for the preliterate, the literate, and the functionally illiterate pupil. If the child is preliterate because he is a young child who has never been in any reading program, the identification of his maturation and his readiness is of primary concern. If an older pupil is preliterate because he has never begun a program of reading and writing, his maturation and readiness may be well-established, but other prereading information may be vital. If the pupil has been struggling with the print of two languages and has been confused by the requirements of both of them, he may be functionally illiterate in English, or in Spanish, or in both languages. For this pupil, a careful assessment of social, linguistic, cultural, and experiential variables is needed before a suitable reading plan can be organized for him.

- **The Young Child Who Speaks Spanish**

Getting ready for reading and learning to read are not separate, isolated tasks, disconnected from the countless learnings that are continuously taking place in the developing, changing life of the child from four to seven years of age. As he masters control of his muscles, he builds the motor skills he needs for reading and writing. When he acquires spatial concepts of directionality, he stores information for future use in handling the sequence of print and its arrangement in sentences and paragraphs. As he observes his surroundings, he enlarges his warehouse of concepts which later serve him well in comprehending written language. With varied opportunities for using manipulative materials, art media, and kinesthetic tools (such as scissors, crayons, pencils, and chalk), he improves his efficiency in coordinating his dominant eye and his preferred hand. He trains his eyes to move together smoothly and to sweep across the page in the direction demanded by the writing system. As oral language competency expands, he uses a more precise sound system and a more sophisticated structural one; he has more words in his vocabulary and has multiple meanings for many of them. This ability to understand and to speak provides him with the necessary background of speech skills which he can bring to the next step in language acquisition—the recognition of this same speech in visual form and the comprehension of it. Throughout the early experiences of the young child, the sorting and sifting of both auditory and visual stimuli, serve as valuable training for subsequent requirements of perceiving and of discriminating among small details of oral and written language as well as for accurate response to the very fine differences which exist among them. This sequence of tasks holds true for all children in all cultures.

A reading program for the young child who speaks only Spanish begins with attention to those prereading skills which he possesses and to those which he may need to acquire or to improve. In this regard, the Spanish speaking child's activities in the primary setting are no different in many respects from those of any child in any reading readiness program. The major decision to consider is language used as an accompaniment, and/or as mediator of meaning, in the daily lessons. For the child who comprehends and speaks Spanish, it appears reasonable to assume that ear training, attention to visual detail, concept acquisition, and language expansion will be accomplished in Spanish as a prelude to an introduction to the writing system of Spanish. It certainly makes sense to bring children from the language which they control in its oral form to the written form of the same language. Because the decision to enter literacy by way of the native language strengths of the Spanish speaking pupil is a social, cultural, and political decision as well as an educational one, the school alone is not always in the ideal position to make an arbitrary selection from among available reading programs.

- **The Child Who Speaks Spanish and English**

It seems incredible that a child who can interpret his world by means of dual language systems could be considered handicapped or viewed as a child with a bilingual problem. Yet, hundreds of deliberations about this child and his reading success or failure center around the negative theme of his disadvantages, his deficiencies, or his deprivations. Traditionally, the school has applied a single yardstick across the broad continuum of language abilities and has concluded that a single reading approach, one which has immersed pupils in an English language based introduction to print, has been the single answer. The complexities of the child's language background may be obscured by this erroneous assumption of homeogeneity of skill acquisition and similarity of language proficiency. It is very important that each child be examined for his specific language strengths across all four bands of language: listening, speaking, reading, and writing in both Spanish and in English. To say that the child is bilingual does not really describe him at all and, therefore, does not identify the language background which he brings to an introductory reading class. The teacher must discover the child's stronger language, as well as the varying degrees of strength among the several language dimensions. Some reasonable questions are these: When the child is listening to language, does he appear to understand better when the material is presented in Spanish or in English? When he is asked to express himself or to respond to questions orally, is he more fluent and more easily understood in English or in Spanish? Or is there any difference; is he equally capable of functioning in either language; is he unable to respond well in either language? There is yet another question: Is his performance in either English or Spanish commensurate with the performance expected for his chronological age and developmental maturity?

After the teacher has ascertained the relative strengths of both languages and has determined the specific encoding and decoding skills, the other customary appraisals of maturation and readiness for reading can be made. It is certainly recognizable that a preliterate pupil could be exceedingly mature and ready to read his native language if an assessment of his dual language background revealed great strength in understanding and speaking Spanish, while at the same time identifying significant weaknesses in his comprehension and fluency in English at a depth sufficient to cope with the demands of a beginning program in English. On the other hand, an appraisal of language dominance might suggest very strong abilities in English and marginal ones in Spanish. Further, there may be differential skill development in listening and speaking proficiencies in one or both languages. To suggest that all pupils who speak Spanish and English are in need of the same kind of reading program in order to achieve success is to ignore, to their detriment and to the frustration of primary teachers, the great range of language differences which call for various program alternatives.

- **The Spanish Speaking Literate Child**

The Spanish speaking child who has learned to read and to write the language which he understands and speaks frequently finds himself in English reading classes. If he is an adequate reader of Spanish and has normal or better intelligence, he usually confounds his teachers with his excellent word recognition skills. As he applies the phonics of his native language with its fairly regular sound-symbol associations, he is able to decode and to call English words rather efficiently. He alters their pronunciation with the delightful flavor of his native speech and often moves blithely on with an approving smile from his teacher who may be mystified by his apparent immediate adjustment in the world of English print. That his instant success is an illusion may not be revealed until the comprehension tasks are presented. Questions concerning the contents of what he has read or inquiries into the meanings of individual words so readily identified may bring few or no accurate responses. The ability to transfer native language reading habits to English, though an immensely important element toward ultimate success in reading English, is at best insufficient and at worst, if long continued and unmonitored in large classes, may be the pupil's total undoing. He may not be seen as a child with some special needs in reading and may be promoted through a reading program because his teachers are not aware of the enormous struggle he is having in understanding what he decodes. He may be able to pronounce the words, but he cannot get meaning from the printed page.

To insure success for the literate Spanish speaking child when he is assigned to the English reading program, it is imperative to place him in a class situation where his competence in the native language can support his efforts to grow and to learn while he is acquiring the necessary language background in oral English for, until the pupil is able to bring meaning to the printed page, he will not take meaning from it. Proper placement would require an assessment of his achievement levels in the various subject areas, his acquired stock of concepts, and his skill proficiencies as demonstrated in Spanish. Prior to entrance into a formal reading program in English, this pupil would need many oral English language opportunities designed on the following bases: 1) richness and clarity of his concepts; 2) his native language abilities in vocabulary, structure, and meaning systems; and 3) the multiple variables implicit in his age and previous school experiences. The Spanish speaking, literate pupil who has enjoyed productive discoveries in his environment and who has information encoded in Spanish and stored for retrieval upon demand, only needs to learn a new labeling system for abundant and accurate concepts already internalized. The experiences unique to the new cultural setting, in which previously undiscovered concepts are available, will have to be encountered and accompanied by the language which explains them. The vocabulary, structure, and meaning system of English, then, may be expected to parallel native language competence if time, patience, and appropriate pacing of the second language are provided. The ability to succeed in reading English will be commensurate with the rate of oral English growth and the ease with which the pupil attaches English labels to concepts he already possesses and/or adds new concepts and new labels.

There are several reading skills which the child can transfer with some gentle direction from the teacher: He can transfer his management of the left-to-right direction common to both writing systems, he can apply his understanding of alphabetic principles, and he can approach English print with a fair measure of confidence since he has coped successfully with reading and writing Spanish. That is, he understands what reading is all about and can now be guided to transfer these basic understandings from Spanish to English. The ultimate level of his reading achievement in English, however, depends upon an orderly and sequential offering of activities to promote the acquisition of specific skills which cannot be expected to accrue automatically. The literate, Spanish speaking pupil has great potential for success in reading English when the reading program takes into account his need for hearing the English sound system, for developing speaking fluency, and for learning the ways that English speech appears in print. Thus, the pupil extends and enlarges his bilingual competencies in the English writing system and enjoys the richness of true bilingualism.

- **The Functionally Illiterate Child**

There are many pupils who have encountered great difficulty in learning to read and write regardless of their language backgrounds. The causes of reading and writing problems are many and often are elusive. The failure to acquire literacy skills when they are expected and demanded in the child's world has far-reaching effects upon his adjustment to school and to his peers. The problem is always with him. Access to subject matter by way of print is closed to him. He often experiences embarrassment and ridicule. He may develop negative attitudes toward all learning because of repeated frustration in his attempts to master the mysterious symbol system with which he has struggled. He finds himself unable to cope with the ever-present, continuing requirement of the educational establishment at all levels. When the stress and pain become too great, he drops out. He may drop out emotionally long before he is legally permitted to do so physically.

The functionally illiterate pupil has an enormous need for individual attention. His inadequate sense of self and his confidence that he can learn both need considerable restoration. If he is very discouraged and distrustful, he may require individual teaching in private sessions where his deficits will not be insensitively broadcast to the rest of the universe. Occasionally, the child can be helped in small groups of pupils whose needs are similar to his. After a careful review of the pupil's school history and other information, the teacher will be able to identify those specific strengths on which the reading program can begin.

At the same time, the teacher must discover the essential skills, abilities, and habits which have been imperfectly developed or are not evident at all. The challenge to both teacher and pupil is one of working together on material that is easy enough to insure a successful experience, appropriate in interest to command respect, and relevant to the pupil's reading needs as identified. It is of great importance that the reading plan begin at a point which will not insult the pupil or be perceived by him as still another assault upon his already dimished ego. Paramount to the design of the lessons is a thorough appraisal of the pupil's oral language functioning and a description of his language development. If he is a child who has been reared in two cultures and has been exposed to two languages, it will be essential to determine his dominant language and to assess the dimensions of both oral and written competency in order that the nurturance of new language skills can build upon those already established. Because the nature of the illiterate pupil's problem is highly complex, it will be vital to gather information relative to many other factors which may have been the causes or the contributors to his lack of reading achievement. Estimates of his intelligence, his health, his sensorimotor abilities, and his prior educational opportunities will assist in planning a reading program at an appropriate level which emphasizes specific learnings required for successful growth. It is discouraging and damaging to a child whose lack of accomplishment in literacy tasks may be rooted in such factors as a high rate of school transfer; few opportunities to receive a developmental, sequential program; confusion resulting from dual language demands; and/or unsuitable materials and approaches in the introductory programs. It is unfortunate for this child to fall from reading readiness to reading remediation a trauma from which a functionally illiterate pupil may never recover.

- **The Dominant Language**

When a pupil's home language is not the same as the language of the instructional program, teachers often face the dilemma of determining the relative strengths of the two languages.

A teacher's practiced eye can become a precision instrument in identifying pupils for whom instruction in English is extremely difficult. Depending upon the composition of the classroom, this teacher can probably select most of the pupils who require an educational plan different from that which is offered to the child who is fully competent in English. For pupils who use both Spanish and English, the teacher must appraise the extent of English language and native language proficiency. It may be necessary for the teacher to recruit a colleague, parent, or member of the community to assist in evaluating the native language of the child.

A simple structured interview technique is useful for determining which language appears stronger. It is important to separate the languages and the specific language competencies of listening, speaking, reading, and writing in each language. Language influences outside the school should be noted as cultural variables.

An example of informal assessment follows:

**THE MARYSVILLE TEST OF LANGUAGE DOMINANCE**

*Directions to Examiner*
1. The child should be tested on two separate occasions by separate examiners unless the teacher is bilingual in English and in the child's native language.
2. The series of questions which follows may be scored as you ask each question.
3. Be certain that you and the pupil are seated in a quiet corner free from distraction.

4. Make every effort to gain the child's complete attention and tell him that you are going to give each question only once.
5. Speak in a conversational tone; do not hurry.
6. Do not give emphasis to any of the material that would distort it for the child.
7. Follow the specific instructions for each set of questions.

*Administration*

Follow the instructions given for each separate page. Use *only* the language of the test. Do not mix Spanish and English.

*Scoring*

Credit one point for each correct response on each of the four language sections: listening, speaking, reading, and writing.

On the Cultural Variables, count the number of responses given as English and count the number of responses given as Spanish.

*Note:* Give credit for each grandparent in Item Five.

*Additional Notes*

1. Young children in preschool and in kindergarten should be given only the *oral* sections (listening and speaking) and the cultural variables.
2. The scores on both languages may be compared to determine the language in which the child appears to function best.
3. Children whose scores do not show any significant differences may be functioning effectively in both the native and the second language.
4. Highly discrepant scores may suggest that a *weak* and a *strong* language coexist, and the teacher may find it more beneficial for the pupil to encourage use of the stronger language system while the other language is being acquired.
5. Rate of school transfer and rural or urban location of the home are not scored, but they do provide descriptive information which may relate to language experience and continuity of school programs.
6. On the Cultural Variables sections only, the items can be adjusted for the level of understanding of students; for example, if the child is not familiar with the word *idioma,* it is perfectly acceptable for the examiner to rephrase the question.

## Test of Listening Comprehension

Ask the pupil to respond to a series of directions. Each response requires only nonverbal communication. Score the responses as correct or incorrect based on the appropriateness and accuracy of the pupil's actions. Discontinue after three consecutive failures.

1. Sit down.
2. Touch your nose.
3. Show me your smallest finger.
4. Hop twice on your right foot.
5. Clap your hands three times.
6. Tap your elbow with the palm of your hand.
7. Make your left hand into a fist.
8. Put your hands behind / in front of your back and lock your thumbs.
9. Select the blue pencil from among those on my desk.
10. Blink your eyes once then keep them closed until I tell you to open them.

Pupil's Name _____ Grade _____ Score ____/10

## Test of Speaking

Ask the pupils the following questions in a *normal* conversational tone and at *normal* speed. Discontinue after three failures. Score responses on the basis of content as appropriate.

1. What is your name?
2. Where do you live?
3. In what grade are you at school?
4. Do you have any brothers and sisters?
5. What work does your father do (engage in)?
6. Are there some special friends you enjoy in your class or in your neighborhood?
7. Let me hear you count to fifty by twos.
8. Where did you used to live before you came to this community?
9. Are you planning to become a teacher, a lawyer, or a musician?
10. If you had your choice of any gift in the world, what would you choose?

Pupil's Name _____ Grade _____ Score ____/10

## Test of Reading

Ask the pupils to read the following items. Score correct only if item is read completely (or letters, characters, symbols of vernacular). Discontinue after three consecutive failures.

1. R, W, X, O, A
2. Me
3. My father
4. Mother and father
5. In my house upstairs
6. The neighborhood is pretty.
7. I have a special friend.
8. Before I lived here, I used to live in Sacramento.
9. When I grow up I'd like to be a doctor or a teacher.
10. I wish I could help my mother, my father, my sisters, my brothers, and everyone in the whole world.

or alternative (just words)
taken from *Speaking Fluency Test*

1. A, T, R, Q, L
2. name
3. live
4. school
5. father
6. friend
7. select
8. clap
9. neighborhood
10. community

Pupil's Name _____ Grade _____ Score ____/10

## Test of Writing

1. Copy these marks:  ⌐   ✕   )   ⊓   /
2. Write these letters: B L M U (or vernacular)
3. Write your first name
4. Write your first and last name
5. Copy this word: Constantinople

*(Continued on page 15.)*

*(Test of Writing continued.)*

**Write from dictation:**
- 6. you
- 7. did
- 8. hands
- 9. touch
- 10. special

(Discontinue after three consecutive failures.)

Pupil's Name _____ Grade _____ Score _____/10

## Cultural Variables
(to be obtained from records and child)

1. Mother's language
   In what language does your mother speak to you? _____

2. Child's characteristic response
   In what language do you answer your mother? _____

3. Father's language
   In what language does your father speak to you? _____

4. Child's characteristic response
   In what language do you answer your father? _____

5. Presence of grandparents
   Does your grandmother and/or grandfather live in your home? (Yes)_____ (No)_____

6. In what language do they speak to you? _____

7. In what language do you answer them? _____

8. What language do you use when speaking to your brothers and sisters? _____
   Are there other people who speak this language living near you? (Yes)_____ (No)_____

9. Location of home (urban/rural)
   Do you live in the town or in the country? _____

10. Rate of school transfer
    How many schools have you attended? _____
    Have you attended school in another country? (Yes)_____ (No)_____

## Prueba de Comprensión Auditiva

Pidale al alumno que siga la siguiente serie de direcciones. Cada respuesta debe ser hecha en silencio. Cuente las respuestas correctas o incorrectas basadas en las acciones del niño. Descontinuelos después de tres errores consecutivos.

1. Siéntate
2. Toca la nariz
3. Enséñame el dedo menique o chiquito
4. Brinca dos veces en el pie derecho
5. Aplauda tres veces
6. Toca el codo con la palma de la mano
7. Cierra la mano izquierda en un puno
8. Pon las manos detras / enfrente de tu espalda y entrelaza los dedos pulgares
9. Escoje un lápiz azul de esos en mi escritorio
10. Parpadeá los ojos una vez y mantengalos cerrados hasta que te diga que los abres

Nombre del alumno _____ Año _____ Calificación ____/10


## Prueba de Hablar

Pregunte a los alumnos las siguientes preguntas en un tono do conversación normal y a una velocidad normal. Descontinuelos despues de tres errores. Califique las respuestas basandose en el contenido.

1. ¿Cómo te llamas?
2. ¿Dónde vives?
3. ¿En qué año estas en la escuela?
4. ¿Tienes hermanos o hermanas?
5. ¿En qué trabaja tu papá?
6. ¿Tienes amigos en tu clase o en tu barrio?
7. Cuenta hasta cincuenta de dos en dos.
8. ¿Dónde viviste antes de venir a esta comunidad?
9. ¿Deseas ser profesor, abogado o músico?
10. Si pudieras tener cualquier regalo en el mundo, ¿qué escogerías?

Nombre del alumno _____ Año _____ Calificación ____/10

### Prueba de Lectura

Digale a los alumnos que lean lo siguiente. Califique correcto solamente si el articulo es leído completamente (o las letras, caracteres, símbolos vernaculos). Descontinuelo despues de tres errores consecutivos.

1. R, W, X, O, A
2. Yo
3. Mi papá
4. Mi mamá y mi papá
5. En el segundo piso de mi casa
6. El vecindario es bonito.
7. Tengo un amigo muy especial.
8. Antes de que viviera aquí, vivia en Sacramento.
9. Cuando crezca me gustaria ser médico o ser maestro.
10. Deseo que pudiera ayudar a mi mamá, mi papá, mis hermanas, mis hermanos y todos en el mundo entero.

o alternative (solo palabras)
tomadas de la Prueba de Hablar

1. A, T, R, Q, L
2. nombre
3. vive
4. escuela
5. papá
6. amigo
7. escoje
8. aplauso
9. vecindario
10. comunidad

Nombre del alumno _____ Año _____ Calificación ____/10

### Prueba de Escribir

1. Copié estos signos:  ⌈   X   )   ⊓   /
2. Escriba estas letras: B L M U (o el vernaculo)
3. Escriba su nombre
4. Escriba su nombre y apellido
5. Copié esta palabra: San Miguel de Allende          *(Continued on page 18.)*

17

*(Test of Writing continued.)*

**Escriba de dictado:**

6. tu

7. hizo

8. manos

9. toca

10. especial

(Discontinuelo despues de tres errores consecutivos)

Nombre del alumno _____Año_____Calificación\_\_\_\_/10

### Variaciones Culturales
(para ser obtenidos de los registros y del nino)

1. Idioma de la mamá
   ¿En qué idioma te habla tu mamá?_____
2. Respuesta caracteristica del niño
   ¿En qué idioma le contestas a tu mamá?_____
3. Idioma del papá
   ¿En qué idioma te habla tu papá?_____
4. Respuesta caracteristica del niño
   ¿En qué idioma le contestas a tu papá?_____
5. Presencia de los abuelos en casa
   ¿Tu abuela o tu abuelo viven en casa contigo o con ustedes?
   (si)_____(no)_____
6. ¿En qué idioma te hablan tus abuelos?_____
7. ¿En qué idioma les contestas?_____
8. ¿En qué idioma hablas a tus hermanos? _____
   ¿Hay otras personas que hablan esta idioma en el barrio cerca de tu casa?  (si)_____(no)_____
9. Localización de la casa (urbana/rural)
   ¿Vives en el pueblo o en el campo?_____
10. Porcentaje de cambios de escuela
    ¿Cuántas escuelas has asistido?_____
    ¿Has asistido a una escuela en otros paises?
    (si)_____(no)_____
    ¿Has asistido a muchas escuelas?
    (si—¿cuántas?_____)
    (no)

*Format for Teacher Use—Items Placed in Appropriate Columns*
(one page for English) (one page for native language)

|     | Listening Comprehension | Speaking Fluency | Reading | Writing | Cultural Variables |
|-----|---|---|---|---|---|
| 1.  |   |   |   |   |   |
| 2.  |   |   |   |   |   |
| 3.  |   |   |   |   |   |
| 4.  |   |   |   |   |   |
| 5.  |   |   |   |   |   |
| 6.  |   |   |   |   |   |
| 7.  |   |   |   |   |   |
| 8.  |   |   |   |   |   |
| 9.  |   |   |   |   |   |
| 10. |   |   |   |   |   |
| SCORE | /10 | /10 | /10 | /10 | /10 |

NAME_____ GRADE_____

Test given in_____

## Teachers' Rating Scales

Classroom teachers can be very keen appraisers of their pupils' language development. They have the advantage of observing pupils in both formal and informal language situations over a relatively long period of time. If specific language behaviors such as comprehension of words in spoken context, accuracy of pronunciation, extent of vocabulary, and other language responses can be noted, then teachers can rate the pupils' performances. If they wish to make comparisons of growth or gains over a period of time, teachers may rate pupils in the fall and again in the spring of the year to see to what degree the program of language development has been effective. Examples of a teacher rating scale in English and Spanish follow.

# MARYSVILLE JOINT UNIFIED SCHOOL DISTRICT
Marysville, California
## Teacher Rating
### Oral Language Assessment for Diagnosis and Planning

Child's Name _____

School _____ School Year _____ Birthdate _____ Grade _____

Indicate the pupil's language competencies by circling the appropriate rating and give your opinion of his *overall* language ability in both receptive (understanding) and expressive (speaking) language. Use criteria listed below as the basis for your rating.

*Rating for Listening Comprehension*
(Receptive Language)

| October | June |
|---|---|
| 1 2 3 4 5 | 1 2 3 4 5 |

*Rating for Speaking Ability*
(Expressive Language)

| October | June |
|---|---|
| 1 2 3 4 5 | 1 2 3 4 5 |

**BASIS FOR RATING:**

| | Understands words in spoken context | Pronunciation | Vocabulary | Correct word order | Complete sentences |
|---|---|---|---|---|---|
| Excellent 5 | Always | Articulates sounds without any errors | Superior | Always | Uses complete sentences and correct word order |
| Good 4 | Usually | Articulates sounds with few errors | Expanded | Usually | Usually uses complete sentences |
| Average 3 | Sometimes | Can be understood but makes errors | Average | Sometimes | Uses sentence fragments |
| Fair 2 | Seldom | Cannot be understood most of the time | Basic | Seldom | Uses only one or two words |
| Poor 1 | Never | Cannot be understood at all | Survival | Never | Uses only gestures |

Recommendations for Pupil's Language Program _____

_____

_____

_____ Teacher _____

DISTRITO UNIFICADO DE LAS ESCUELAS DE MARYSVILLE
Marysville, California
*Calificación del Maestro*
**Evaluación de Lenguaje Oral para Diagnosticar y Planear**

Nombre del alumno _____ Fecha de nacimiento _____

Escuela _____ Año escolar _____ Grado _____

Ponga un círculo alrededor del número que significa la propia calificación de lenguaje para este alumno y dé su opinión sobre la habilidad del niño (a) en lenguaje receptiva y lenguaje expresiva. Use el criterio siguiente para su calificación.

| *Calificación de Oír* (Lenguaje Receptiva) | | *Calificación de Habilidad en Hablar* (Lenguaje Expresiva) | |
|---|---|---|---|
| *Octubre* | *Junio* | *Octubre* | *Junio* |
| 1 2 3 4 5 | 1 2 3 4 5 | 1 2 3 4 5 | 1 2 3 4 5 |

*BASE de CALIFICACIÓN:*

| | Comprende palabras habladas | Pronunciación | Vocabulario | Orden de palabras en un modo correcto | Frases completas |
|---|---|---|---|---|---|
| Excelente 5 | Siempre | Pronuncia sin error | Sobresaliente | Siempre | Usa las frases completas y la orden de palabras correctamente |
| Bueno 4 | Casi todo el tiempo | Pronuncia con pocos errores | Superior | Casi todo el tiempo | Usa las frases completas casi todo el tiempo |
| Regular 3 | A veces | Se puede entenderle pero hay errores | Regular | A veces | Usa las frases incompletas |
| Adecuado 2 | Casi nunca | Casi no se puede entenderle todo el tiempo | Adecuado | Casi nunca | Usa una o dos palabras |
| Mínimo 1 | Nunca | Nunca se puede entenderle | Mínimo | Nunca | Usa señas |

Recomendaciones para el programa de lenguaje del alumno _____

Maestro(a) _____

There are several other measures presently available for language appraisal:

1. Dos Amigos Verbal Language Scales, 1974 (Grades 1–4)
   Academic Therapy Publications
   1539 Fourth Street
   San Rafael, California 94901

2. Bilingual Syntax Measure, 1973 (Grades K–2)
   Harcourt Brace Jovanovich
   Testing Department
   757 Third Avenue
   New York, New York 10017

3. James Language Dominance Test, 1974 (Grades K–1)
   Learning Concepts
   Speech Division
   2501 N. Lamar
   Austin, Texas 78705

4. Spanish-English Language Dominance Assessment, 1972 (Grades 1–2)
   Professor Bernard Spolsky
   The University of New Mexico
   1805 Roma NE
   Albuquerque, New Mexico 87106

Chapter 2

## READING PROGRAM ALTERNATIVES FOR THE SPANISH SPEAKING CHILD

- **Literacy in a Second Language**

The rationale which supports a program of immediate introduction to English reading and writing would appear to be sound. It is certainly true that Spanish speaking pupils who expect to survive and to compete in the classroom must acquire strong English language proficiency and excellent literacy skills. Since the ability to read English textbooks and workbooks is a primary requirement for academic success in the content areas of science, social science, mathematics, and other subjects, pupils who cannot function in English print find access to these fields of knowledge blocked. The school is print oriented and, after the primary grades, makes few provisions for means of instruction beyond reading and writing assignments. Not only are the day to day activities carried largely by written language, but written achievement tests are also the yardsticks by which pupil and, at times, teacher competencies are judged. There can be no argument offered against the educational objective of bringing Spanish speaking pupils along in English, as rapidly and as efficiently as possible across all the language arts—listening, speaking, reading, and writing. Without question, pupils who live in a predominantly English speaking country must develop the best English language mastery that is within their power to acquire. There is, however, considerable room for discussion of the underachievement of Spanish speaking pupils for the past century, and there is good reason to examine current classroom practices in second language literacy.

Reading programs as they are presently designed for native speakers of English are totally unsuited to the reading needs of native Spanish speaking pupils who are burdened with an unfamiliar sound and symbol system. They have been provided with too few or too inconsistent periods of prereading activities. They have found little in the cultural content of reading material that makes sense to them. They have not been given sufficient time for new language skills to grow but have been expected to move along at the same pace with their native English speaking classmates. There has been scarcely any provision for dealing with the interference which they receive from their native

Spanish. The grinding, corrosive effect of repeated failure and frustration has made reading, in particular, and school, in general, a very unsatisfactory experience for hundreds of thousands of these children. The traditional reading programs must be reexamined and reevaluated in the light of today's evidence of the reading failure of Spanish speaking pupils. It is essential to identify program inadequacies which create stumbling blocks for pupils for whom English is not a native language. Reading programs in English must be appraised critically to discover what characteristics should be retained because they are supportive of the Spanish speaking child's literacy attempts. There is great need, also, to recognize features which must be discarded or radically changed because they are destructive of the child's efforts.

- **Traditional Reading Approaches in English**

The *basal reader method* is an organized presentation of sequential material in graded readers, workbooks, and supplementary lessons. A key ingredient in this basic reading method is a very complete and carefully prepared teachers' guide for each level of difficulty. A competent teacher can follow the detailed instructions in the manual and can offer many interesting, productive activities in reading for the majority of the native speakers of English in the classroom. Basal readers have been skillfully written by able people who understand the literacy process and the interests of elementary pupils very well. For decades, millions of school age children have mastered the mysteries of the English language system of print through the basal reader approach. Yet, there are some pitfalls inherent for the Spanish speaking child. Some of the perils lie in the lockstep, graded nature of the readers themselves; other difficulties can be found in the unrealistic pacing of the lessons for pupils who are not native to English; many problems are evident in the lack of oral language preparation prior to the introduction of print; and conflicts in the cultural content are frequent for pupils whose experiences and values differ. Because the program is arranged in a hierarchical order of difficulty of reading and writing skills, the written vocabulary and language patterns at each level may be narrow, limiting the literary quality of the materials to which the pupils are exposed. For Spanish speaking pupils, who may be dependent upon reading instruction to enhance their oral language skills, the basal approach may prove sterile and unstimulating. Further, there is a tacit supposition of language control on an oral level minimally comparable to a six-year-old's ability to understand and to speak. Such an assumption is based upon at least six years of exposure to and practice with the sounds, the structures, the vocabulary, and the meanings of English. Even when native English speakers have had this time for developing oral competency, there is often need for reading teachers to extend the time and to provide for further language acquisition before pupils are moved too rapidly into print. Consider, then, the Spanish speaking child and his relatively short periods of intermittent association with English. For this child, the language and content of the basal approach may need both thoughtful revision and careful monitoring to overcome its deficits.

The *linguistic method* is one which introduces the patterns of language in their written forms according to a systematic, regular plan which controls speech-print discrepancies by a precise ordering of the lessons. Regular sound-symbol associations, simple spelling patterns, and short sentences are first presented and practiced before the many speech-print inconsistencies of English are offered. This approach emphasizes that print is a representation of speech and draws the pupil's attention to the relationships which exist between speech and print. Linguistic methods vary among themselves in many respects but share a common concern for decoding or reconstructing print into the speech which such print represents. For the Spanish speaking child's first experience with written English, materials and methods based upon linguistic principles may lead him along a safe, reliable path to reading English and to understanding many of its linguistic features. The beginning reader is likely to develop a fair degree of confidence from his success in analyzing consistent language and spelling patterns arranged in short, manageable units. One of the major criticisms of linguistic methods is that content must be contrived and unnatural in order to adhere rigidly to the language patterns as introduced. Thus, all the short vowel utterances used in a single lesson may create stories devoid of interest or excitement for the reader. For any child (but particularly for the Spanish speaking child), there is not much possibility for transfer of reading skills, so narrowly circumscribed, to the broad needs of reading materials in mathematics, science, social sciences, or other subjects. There is also the danger that many of the sounds of English represented by the written arrangements may be quite alien to the child's ears. The short *i* and short *u* in consonant-vowel-consonant patterns—bit, hit, but, hut—are examples of which teachers must be aware. If the Spanish speaking child is fortunate enough to be immersed in a stimulating oral language program—one which provides him with ample opportunity to listen to a full range of speech patterns and to unrestricted vocabulary and structures—the acquisition of primary reading skills as a decoding process by way of this approach, appears to be among the best of the second language reading alternatives.

*Phonic methods* are based upon certain principles of speech-print relationships. There are two general approaches to the teaching of these rules governing the written language of English. One begins with individual letters and sounds in combinations and the other introduces whole words which can be analyzed into their phonic elements. It is a method which depends largely upon the oral language ability of the learner and upon his auditory skills in perceiving and discriminating among the fine distinctions of spoken English. Some native speakers have great difficulty learning to read by means of phonics methods, particularly if they have poorly integrated auditory experiences in language. Attempting to learn to read English through phonics can be a disaster for the Spanish speaking child. There are so many sounds in English that have no phonological reality in Spanish. There is no sound of *h*, no final *nk*, no initial *s* consonant blends. The pronunciations of many letters—the *j*, the *d*, the *v* and the *r*—in many positions within words in English are significantly different even though the visual appearances are the same. There are also many exceptions to phonics generalizations which create confusion for pupils who have learned to apply phonic principles. It has been estimated that the English speech-print correspondence rules apply only 85 percent of the time. English speaking pupils who can benefit from phonics approaches are no doubt able to make the most of this percentage of reliability; but for the Spanish speaking child, the complexities of discovering new language sounds, of installing them among his known repertoire, of associating them with their written forms, of grasping meanings from them, and of using any rule generated are truly impossible tasks. The hazards of overdoing phonics are well known in reading circles. The numbers of English speaking pupils who can recognize letter-sound relationships in isolation but who fail to ever get them together for use in actual reading are sadly documented in research. For the Spanish speaking child to acquire the phonic skills necessary to unlock English print, the task may be burdensome and the returns may be minimal in terms of reading accomplishment.

The *language experience method* is based upon the fact that a person acquires language as he experiences a specific environment. The words and expressions he uses to explain and to recall such experiences become his spoken language. When a person is developmentally mature and psychologically ready to add the written forms of language, oral language and previous experience form the basis for reading. This approach moves through what the pupil has encountered and *thought* about to what he can *say* about it to what the teacher can *write* about it and, finally, to what the learner himself can read; that is, transform back into his personal language and thought by reading. Finally, the child masters the handwriting skills necessary to write his own material. A language experience introduction to literacy provides the pupil with the fairly straightforward relationships among thinking, listening, comprehending, reading, and writing. Written language is viewed as a visual form of speech. English speaking pupils of primary school age bring a background of years of experience *and* language to this method and often benefit enormously from an approach which focuses on their personal worlds. In spite of criticism that the reading vocabularies of learners are not systematically controlled or that the acquisition of reading skills is not sequentially organized, both teachers and pupils have discovered great delight in learning to read by language experience. There is much to recommend this approach for the Spanish speaking child. As art activities, story times, field trips, and other opportunities for experiences mediated by English are provided, the child develops meanings and language which can then make sense to him in written forms. He is using personal content which consists of information labeled in oral English and understood as it appears in print. He can be a successful reader of English immediately if the pace is appropriate and the language experiences are suitable for his oral control of English.

There are other approaches to the teaching of reading. Among these are programed instruction, individualized reading, augmented Roman alphabet, and teaching machines. Like all methods, these are useful and productive for some children when used by skillful teachers and when they fit the language backgrounds of pupils. Any approach to the teaching of reading English, no matter how promising, must be modified for use with the Spanish speaking child whose language and culture differ in so many ways from the content and form of these methods. Educators who must design effective reading programs for Spanish speaking children in classrooms of English speaking countries must consider thoughtfully the many difficulties of reading in a second language and select from among the available materials and methods those which will contribute positively to reading achievement. It may well be that an eclectic approach—one which uses characteristics of language experience, linguistics, and various other methods—will be needed to bring the Spanish speaking child to literacy in English. The burden of decision lies with educators who have a pressing responsibility to reverse the tragic statistics of underachievement, overageness, dropout rates, and failures of Spanish speaking children in public education.

- **Literacy in the Native Language**

It is reasonable to assume that a Spanish speaking pupil should read first the language which he has acquired in his home. The long period of infancy and preschool years has offered thousands of hours of sound saturation, available language models, and opportunities for imitation. The normal school-age child can reproduce the Spanish sound system with ease and fluency. He controls most of the structures he needs to create meaningful speech utterances, he possesses a vocabulary and a storehouse of meanings commensurate with the language experiences to which he has been exposed, and he has internalized a system of oral language which explains his world and which serves him adequately. Like his English speaking peer who enters school at this same developmental stage, the Spanish speaking child has had to deal only with oral language. Upon entering the classroom, the child must begin to acquire skills in using the conventions of written language which represent the spoken language of the family and community into which he has been born.

For the child who speaks Spanish, the tasks of learning to read and to write Spanish can be most satisfying and productive endeavors. The pupil has information which makes sense to him, and he has it encoded and stored in oral language which he knows. He now has to add to this knowledge a single new dimension, the written representation of Spanish. Instead of having to deal simultaneously with two or three unknowns—English speech, print, and referents—he merely has to memorize the visual symbols of the Spanish writing system and associate them with the auditory symbols of Spanish speech. He must learn the code and must grow in his ability to decipher the code efficiently. Fortunately for the Spanish speaking child, there is a fairly regular and consistent relationship between written and spoken Spanish. The speech-print correspondence, though not perfect, is dependable enough to create a sense of self-confidence in the child and belief in his own feelings of competence as a beginning reader.

Coming to grips with the system of sound-symbol relationships is only the first step for the Spanish speaking child. It is a significant one, however, as he improves in his abilities to hear his native Spanish and to see its representation in visual form. The task of comprehending what he has decoded is more difficult because it involves the multiple factors of intellect, experience, and oral language background. His success in both decoding and comprehending written Spanish is influenced by his sensitivity to the sound elements of his native language and his storehouse of information encoded in Spanish. He uses his facility in oral language to make meaning of written Spanish. Like readers in any language, he takes away from a printed page information commensurate with what he brings to that page.

- **Traditional Reading Approaches in Spanish**

In Spanish speaking countries throughout the world, pupils in the elementary grades learn to read by means of one or several major approaches. One such approach, *el método onomatopoéico,* aims at the systematic development of constant auditory associations for letters and sounds based upon something or someone in the pupil's environment; for example, the vowel sound of *i* is taught in connection with the squeal of a mouse—*iii.* The sound of a train whistle is called to mind every time the pupil encounters the *u,* etc. Each phonemic element has its identity within this method and as pupils learn to make these individual associations, they acquire skills in decoding the printed words and in making them recognizable in spoken form. The consonants are often repeated in words and phrases to create an alliterative effect. *El túnel de Tomás está en el monte.* After the pupils are able to make accurate and quick associations, they are encouraged to analyze word parts and identify syllables. The materials are arranged to provide for the recognition of the sounds in several positions within words and sentences—initial, ending, and medial—so that pupils receive practice in discovering the same sound-symbol relationship in a variety of symbol environments—vowels preceded by consonants, consonant clusters and vowel combinations, consonants between vowels, and vowels in combination.

*El método alfabético* begins with the names of the letters of the alphabet. Usually the vowels are presented first and then the consonants. The pupil is then shown how the consonants and vowels go together to create syllables and then how syllables can be joined to create words; for example, *ma . . no—mano; be . . be—bebe; mo . . no—mono.* It is a synthetic method, one which requires pupils to put word elements together to construct whole words. Pupils are expected to use the letter names to spell the words created; for example, *eme a ene o—mano.* Although many Spanish speaking pupils have learned to read by *el método alfabético,* this approach has been criticized as dull, repetitive, and tedious. Further, the blending of isolated letters into syllables is frequently complicated by the retention of the letter name as another letter is added; e.g., b—be and a—*ba* may be blended as *bea* instead of *ba.* Some letters are very clumsy to put together in this way and may result in considerable confusion for the beginning pupil. It has been suggested that *el método alfabético* is more comfortable for the teachers who can follow an explicit plan to guide them in presenting the initial reading lessons to primary pupils. But the convenience of the teachers is not a legitimate reason for selecting any method.

El *método fónico o fonético* emphasizes the sounds which the letters of the alphabet represent and is not directly concerned with the names of the letters. The pupils must learn all the sounds represented by all the letters and letter combinations. This approach, like the alphabetic method, is a part-whole system which requires pupils to synthesize word elements, sounds, and syllables into whole words. It differs, however, because the conventional letter names are ignored and the letters are identified purely on the basis of the sounds they represent. The consonants retain their full phonic value and do not need a vowel sound in order to be named. Spelling activities are not included or even desired in the introductory lessons. There are teachers who have used *el método fónico* with considerable success, particularly with pupils who have good auditory skills and who appear to learn best through the auditory channel. Some of the sounds are difficult to pronounce in isolation, however, and many teachers have noted problems their pupils have encountered with sounds represented by *la b, p, q,* and *l.*

*El método de palabras generadoras* is a whole word method. The teacher presents entire words for the pupils to see; he tells the pupils what the words are; he illustrates their meanings; he asks the pupils to pronounce them; and finally, he expects the pupils to memorize them. At this introductory stage, the words are presented as if they are entire units which cannot be divided. The next step, however, is one in which the pupils analyze the words they have learned and then identify the basic parts which have gone together to make up the words. First, the pupils identify the syllables; then, they identify the sound elements found in each syllable; and finally, they learn the letters which represent the sound elements. This process is an analytic one which gives the pupils the opportunity to see the relationships which exist between letters and sounds, between sounds and syllables, and between syllables and words. When pupils have taken words apart and have been successful at an analysis of word elements, they are then taught to put the parts back together in a reconstituted whole and to create new words by arranging syllables they have learned in different combinations. Finally, they are taught to group words they have learned or created into phrases and sentences. *El método de palabras generadoras* requires the pupils to apply both analysis and synthesis as they progress in learning to read.

Some of the criticism of this whole word approach has centered around the question of who does the analysis and the synthesis. It has been argued that the teacher will be the one to identify syllables, point out sound elements, and give the letters their names. According to this view, the pupil is merely a passive recipient of information. Another difficulty frequently mentioned is that of the enormous burden of writing whole words before adequate skills in handwriting have had time to develop. Perhaps the most vigorous objection comes from the suggestion to create new words from syllables as discovered. Often, this practice results in stilted, artificial expressions, and the inclusion of rare words quite foreign to the vocabulary and interest of children.

*El método global* consists of the teaching of reading and writing by means of whole words or complete sentences without ever analyzing the component elements, syllables, or letters. According to this approach, the content which has meaning and interest for children is the most important factor in learning to read. Practices which encourage sound-symbol relationships and syllabic structuring are avoided as activities which produce ambiguities and absurdities. The global method claims to help the pupil follow his natural tendencies with spontaneity and with feeling. The reading lesson is usually introduced by encouraging the pupils to draw some things which they can talk about. The teacher writes what the pupils have said, and the children are encouraged to copy it. The classroom expressions *silencio; buenas tardes, niños; hasta mañana,* and *niños* are written on cards for the children to copy. Each day's lesson can be developed according to a particular theme and the vocabulary relevant to the day's theme can be presented. Flash cards containing suitable words and expressions are made up for practice and review. Items in the classroom environment are labeled for the pupils to see and to read. The teacher uses drawing, talking, copying, reading, and writing together so that lessons are personally interesting and rewarding to each pupil. The children keep individual notebooks of their work and get a great deal of pleasure from seeing their accomplishments grow as the year progresses.

*El método global* has many features which will delight and motivate young children. Centers of interest, games, pictures, and drawings, all serve to create a stimulating atmosphere for pupils. Though there are major emphases on both the visual and the motor skills, there is little or no attention focused on the auditory dimensions of reading. The pupils do listen as the teacher presents lessons or reads what has been written on a drawing or flash card, but there is never a requirement to connect speech sounds to written representations except in whole words or sentences. The pupils do not acquire a system for unlocking unfamiliar words beyond the visual clues and visual patterns which they have, hopefully, remembered. The daily requirements of drawing and writing can prove difficult for some pupils whose visual-motor control and coordination may be minimal. There is little or no restriction on new written material and no guarantee that sufficient review can be provided to help pupils retain their reading vocabularies through systematic practice or drill. The demands on the teacher are great as he must prepare and arrange new stimuli constantly. Further, he must be extremely well organized in order to keep track of how each pupil is progressing and what problems, if any, each is meeting along the way. In spite of these disadvantages, *el método global* does provide the beginning reader with the practical realization that there is a functional relationship between what is said and what is written.

*El método ecléctico* consists of procedures which are both analytic and synthetic in nature. Essentially, this method selects and uses a variety of features from several methods in order to provide the best learning opportunities for the pupils. For the beginning pupil, there are preparatory exercises to promote skills in spatial organization, visual-motor coordination, auditory discrimination, attention, memory, and oral language. Then the vowels are presented and pupils are urged to practice the sound, the letter name, and the handwriting skills needed to form the letters in both the lower and uppercase forms. The joining of two vowels to form diphthongs may also be taught at this initial stage in the reading program. Next, the consonant sounds, letters, and written forms are taught. The formation of syllables and the analysis of words into syllables are both used to provide practice for the pupils. Pupils are taught to make sound-symbol associations, to take dictation, to copy, to create new words, to visualize the shapes of the letters, to identify the sounds represented by letters, to write the letter forms, and to understand the speech-print relationships of the primary materials.

The eclectic method is sufficiently varied to accommodate many different kinds of pupils and several different styles of teaching. Because the eclectic label applies not only to the method, but also to materials and to many other aspects of organization of the reading plan, there is potential for greater flexibility in the program. The teacher is able to offer individual pupils selected activities which are appropriate for their strengths and weaknesses.

The various approaches used to teach reading to Spanish speaking pupils in Spanish speaking countries have all enjoyed some measure of success with some pupils. As in teaching reading in English, a method is effective in direct proportion to the skill of the teacher who uses it. Promising approaches can fail in the hands of a poorly trained, indifferent teacher while a method with many inherent weaknesses may be applied successfully by a knowledgeable, supportive one. An overview of the traditional methods is of interest to teachers in the United States as new considerations are being given to the possibilities of native language and second langauge literacy in Spanish-English bilingual education programs.

Among the few programs in English speaking countries where children who speak Spanish have been taught to read the native language, there have been important questions raised over the suitability of reading materials imported from abroad for use in literacy programs of the United States. A major problem has been the Spanish language competence of the teacher. Teacher guides from Spain or from Mexico assume a certain degree of familiarization with methods, materials, and language of the country. The pupils' books often contain religious or political ideas inimical to educational practices in a democracy. The pacing of instruction is usually inappropriate for pupils who are not immersed in a monolingual, Spanish setting, but rather are constantly shifting back and forth between the English of their schools and the Spanish of their families. In an English speaking community there are few opportunities to try newly acquired literacy skills by reading street signs, restaurant menus, or storefront advertising and pupils encounter interference from English daily. For these and other reasons, United States teachers have had to modify materials intended for Spanish speaking pupils in Spanish speaking countries and have had to use them cautiously. Teachers who have limited fluency in Spanish have been reluctant to use them at all. Others have become highly dependent upon the skills of paraprofessionals, parent volunteers, and colleagues.

With the recent establishment and funding of various Spanish-English bilingual programs in schools of the United States, there have been numerous efforts to develop materials and methods for teaching Spanish reading and writing which are more suitable for pupils who are living in two cultural and linguistic environments. These publications have been prepared expressly for Spanish speaking children who are enrolled in schools where the customary medium of instruction is English. The special learning problems of these pupils have been considered by the authors of prereading activities, games, charts, manipulative items, reading skill lessons, and readers. From an historical and educational point of view, programs of native language literacy for Spanish speaking pupils represent a major curriculum change, one which will have an impact on the design of literacy programs in English as well.

- **Selecting Materials**

Teachers must select or create materials for programs of Spanish reading on the basis of criteria by which relevant and appropriate materials can be identified. Crucial to the selection of materials is the language competency of the teacher who will be expected to use them. Materials must also be chosen to fit the instructional objectives of the reading program. Other considerations are the ages and interest levels of the pupils, the social-cultural content, the support services available to teachers, and the cost. A checklist for evaluating materials follows. It is not all-inclusive, but does contain many of the major questions raised by teachers, parents, and the community.

CRITERIA FOR SELECTING MATERIALS (8)

Title_____ Publisher_____
Type of Material (workbook, textbook, library book, other)_____
Grade Level_____ Evaluator_____

|  | Yes | No | Non-related |
|---|---|---|---|
| 1. Teacher competencies |  |  |  |
|    a. Do the materials demand a high degree of teacher competency? | ___ | ___ | ___ |
|    b. Do the materials require language proficiency in the vernacular of the learner? | ___ | ___ | ___ |
|    c. Do the materials lend themselves to good use by inexperienced as well as experienced teachers? | ___ | ___ | ___ |
|    d. Are the materials suitable for use by teachers who have varied teaching styles and temperaments? | ___ | ___ | ___ |
| 2. Objectives of the instructional program |  |  |  |
|    a. Are the materials consistent with the natural order of language learning? | ___ | ___ | ___ |
|    b. Do activities proceed from listening comprehension and speaking fluency to reading and writing? | ___ | ___ | ___ |
|    c. Are the materials organized in a speech-to-print direction which provides for oral language development sufficient to support written language? | ___ | ___ | ___ |
|    d. Do the materials respect the vernacular of the pupils, appreciate the sound and structural conflicts, and provide for the use of the native language strengths of the learner? | ___ | ___ | ___ |

3. Age of the pupils
   a. Are the materials appropriate for the age at which reading English as a second language is begun?
   b. Are the content, situation, and language suitable for the maturity of the pupils?
   c. Are the situations and stories of interest to the pupils?
   d. Are the motivational possibilities of the materials realistic?
4. Time available for use
   a. Are the classroom realities of time considered in the skills development?
   b. Is use of teacher time efficient and economical?
   c. Is pupil time demanded on a uniform or individual basis?
   d. May pupils adjust time allowances without too much difficulty in managing the materials?
5. Provision for individual learners
   a. Do materials provide for differential aptitudes of pupils, (intelligence, experience, maturity, health, resistance to fatigue, etc.)?
   b. Are there materials which will interest both boys and girls?
   c. Do the materials offer practice as needed for slow and fast learners?
   d. Can the materials accommodate visual, auditory, and kinesthetic styles of learning?
   e. Are special strengths and weaknesses in reading skills provided for?
6. Articulation status
   a. Do the materials offer sequential and orderly progression through the grades within an individual school program?
   b. Do the materials provide background for reading at higher levels of instruction?
   c. Do the skills build the basic and specialized abilities to deal with subject matter in the content areas?
   d. Are the materials generally consistent with those used in other programs within the geographic region or nation?
7. Services available to assist teachers
   a. Does the school or district provide consultants to help teachers use materials well?
   b. Are there resource teachers and supervisors in the schools for immediate services when needed?
   c. Do the commercial publishing houses offer assistance in implementing programs with the materials?
   d. Are there workshops, institutes, and continuing education programs in which teachers may receive additional training in the use of the materials?
   e. Are college and university resources available to assist in research and evaluation of programs in which the materials are to be used?
8. Ease of handling and attractiveness
   a. Are there relevant and effective charts, filmstrips, flashcards, pictures and other instructional materials available to support the basic program?
   b. Are the aids readily accessible, easy to use, and interesting to the pupils?
9. Cultural content
   a. Is the content of these materials culturally authentic?
   b. Are the people, events, and situations portrayed in a fair, factual manner free from stereotyping?
   c. Do the materials promote an appreciation of the richness of cultural diversity?
10. Supplementary materials
    a. Are there correlated materials (games, records, workbooks, study sheets) which will offer reinforcement and review as needed?
    b. Do the additional materials extend the skills of rapid learners and offer acceleration as well as enrichment opportunities?

11. Cost
   a. Are the costs realistic in terms of the financial capabilities of the school district? ___  ___  ___
   b. Are the costs consistent with the expectations of the community? ___  ___  ___
   c. Do the costs represent a reasonable investment in the literacy skills of the pupils? ___  ___  ___
   d. Have costs been considered from the viewpoint of replacement of materials, maintenance, and upkeep? ___  ___  ___

- **Social-Cultural Content**

Fundamental skills in reading can be carried by a variety of materials. Pupils who speak Spanish can learn about their history and heritage from materials which tell about Spanish speaking people and events. They can acquire and practice skills of remembering, reasoning, summarizing, or analyzing content which carries information of relevance and of importance to their ethnicity. If the pupils are learning to read in their native Spanish, then authentic stories written by Spanish speaking authors about real or imaginary situations provide a framework for skills development. If, however, pupils are coming to literacy by means of the second language, English, then the ethnic content can be adapted and changed to include experiences from the social and cultural environment in which the Spanish speaking pupils live. Ricardo Garcia points out the potential for using the pupils' own resources for reading and writing. He suggests photographs of the *barrio,* rhythms of recorded music, ethnic games, special foods, and collections of humor as rich reservoirs of content which can be provided in either language *(2).*

Chapter 3

## THE DEVELOPMENTAL NATURE OF LITERACY

- **Literacy Is a Task for Middle Childhood**

The highly demanding work of learning to read and to write is not a requirement of infancy or of early childhood. The young child must develop many prior skills before he can undertake the complex, neurological task of understanding written language and of expressing himself through its medium. Yet, there appears to exist a pervasive tendency to consider learning to read and to write as separate, isolated activities which the child engages in simply because he is enrolled in a school setting. This view of the place of literacy in the child's growth often results in an introduction to many of the formal aspects of reading and writing at a time which may be considerably out of harmony with the child's developmental timetable.

Havighurst *(3)* has reminded educators that literacy skills are certainly developmental in nature and that they are expected to emerge during the period of middle childhood. He further cautions that while successful achievement of each developmental task along the way to full maturity results in the person's happiness and in his ability to advance to higher, more demanding levels, failure leads to difficulty with later tasks and to comcomitant frustration, maladjustment, and unhappiness.

The period of middle childhood spans the years approximately from age six to ten years, a relatively long period of time in which to present the introductory concepts and to practice the skills which result in the establishment of habits of literacy. It is important to note that middle childhood does range over several years in the child's development. Of critical concern, also, is the fact that all children are not at the same stages in physical and/or intellectual growth even though they may share the same chronological ages. Thus, in the middle childhood period, some children at age six (or earlier) may be fully mature and ready to begin a program of reading and writing; others may not be mature and ready until seven, eight, or nine years of age. Like all children, the Spanish speaking child must be considered within this framework of development, maturation, and readiness as his literacy needs are examined.

Several influences from elements within the developing child and from sources outside of him may contribute positively or negatively to his growth. The Spanish speaking pupil follows an orderly progression of growth according to his own inner timetable of maturation. Like all normal children, he has reached the significant milestones of sitting, standing, walking, talking, and adapting on the basis of his innate capacity to do so and the cultural expectations placed upon him. Though this progression may be altered slightly by specific environmental conditions which may enhance or delay development, his physical maturity is a function of his own personal uniqueness.

For the developmental task of learning to read, the teacher must determine the extent to which each pupil is physically mature enough to benefit from introductory lessons designed to present the prereading skills. For all children from any language community, there is the commonly shared requirement of maturation of the central nervous system and the brain. The classroom teacher can informally observe a pupil's level of maturation by noting how skillfully he manages a variety of sensorimotor tasks in ordinary classroom situations. The teacher may consider skillfulness or clumsiness in both the gross motor activities (walking, running, hopping, skipping) and in the fine motor activities (copying, cutting, stringing beads). The teacher's practiced eye will also serve as a precision instrument for appraising the pupil's skills in matching shapes, objects, letters, and numerals. His ability to remember a sequence of forms, pictures, or objects can also be readily observed. If a more systematic method of assessment is preferred, the teacher may use one of the many excellent inventories of developmental tasks which include items to sample proficiency in eye-motor coordination, visual-motor skills, and usual-perceptual abilities.

One essential ingredient in estimating the maturational levels of a Spanish speaking pupil is that he be given instructions for tasks to be performed in the language which he understands. Adaptation of examiner directions as needed will create useful tools out of existing developmental measures designed for the English speaking child. For example, to assess gross motor coordination, the teacher (or a Spanish speaking colleague) may ask: *¿puedes brincar?* (can you hop?); *¿ puedes pararte con un pie?* (can you stand on one foot?); *¿puedes saltar de aquí hasta allí?* (can you jump from here up to there?) To estimate visual-motor abilities (copying, cutting, and other fine muscle tasks), the teacher or a Spanish speaking colleague may direct the pupil: *Quiero que cortes en esta línea con las tijeras* (I want you to cut on this line with the scissors); *quiero que hagas dos círculos como estos* (I want you to make two circles like these); *quiero que metas estas bolitas en esta cinta* (I want you to put these little beads on this string); etc. The visual memory and visual perceptual items can be easily adapted in Spanish and the gross auditory abilities such as perceiving and discriminating differences and similarities among *common* environmental sounds require only the translation of instructions to the pupil: *Cierra* *los ojos y me dices lo que oyes.* (Close your eyes, and tell me what you hear.) When the teacher attempts to assess the fine auditory skills of perceiving and of discriminating among speech sounds, however, the language items may be drawn from Spanish if the child's native language is Spanish and if Spanish has been retained as the stronger language despite the influences of other language learnings. If the teacher is attempting to assess the English language background, then, the presentation of language tasks in English is appropriate. The kind of information sought will depend upon the type of reading program offered. For example, if the only reading program offered is in English, then, the child's control of English connected discourse is essential. On the other hand, if the pupil is to enter a Spanish reading program, an estimate of the child's native language strengths is of greater importance. As a teacher is gathering information relative to a pupil's developmental maturity and language, he may also discover the child's ability to sustain attention, to persist in the completion of a task, and to cope with the stress of new demands.

At the prereading level, teachers are vitally concerned with the discovery of the maturation of pupils and also with the identification of their readiness to read. Readiness refers to the adequacy of the child's physical, social, experiential, emotional, and psychological potential for engaging in a specific activity. Readiness to read may be viewed as the optimal stage of a child's development for beginning reading instruction. Although the principle of readiness must necessarily be examined within the context of his maturity, maturation and readiness are not identical constructs. It is essential to differentiate between a pupil's maturation and his readiness as well as to recognize that while maturation is controlled by the inner timetable of the child, his readiness can be nurtured by conditions outside him. Teachers are generally very skillful at making this distinction by carefully observing their pupils in a variety of informal situations and by periodically testing them in a more formal setting. This distinction is especially significant for the Spanish speaking child in U.S. schools because, ordinarily, the principle of readiness has been applied to the specific activity of readiness to read English.

Perhaps one of the best predictors of readiness to read is the level of the child's language development. His skill in hearing and reproducing the sound system is fundamental to the acquisition of vocabulary and to the control of language structures. An appraisal of the Spanish speaking child's readiness to read may be made on the basis of the language he controls in its oral form. Assessment can be expanded to determine the dual readinesses of reading Spanish and of reading English. One of the major discrepancies in the use of the traditional readiness measure designed for use with English speaking pupils is that the test content is often unfamiliar and irrelevant to pupils whose native language is Spanish. The obtained data may suggest that the mature pupil is quite unready to read English but if a measure of his Spanish language competence is taken, the results may indicate adequate or better readiness to read Spanish. In evaluating a Spanish speaking child's readiness to read Spanish, the measures applied and the instruments used to obtain any information should consist of appropriate items drawn from the universe of Spanish language content.

A developmental view of literacy requires educators to examine these two conditions: *maturation* and *readiness*. The maturation principle and its implications for teaching young children apply to all pupils with the same impartiality. Immature pupils cannot be made mature ahead of their schedules and must be given patience, time, and opportunities for growth. The readiness principle and its implications for teaching children should apply only to mature pupils who may or may not be adequately prepared to undertake the specific task of learning to read a particular language. For mature Spanish speaking pupils, readiness can be nurtured and enhanced by good teaching, once the specific nature of the reading plan is identified. Among the prereading skills which are amenable to positive classroom practices are the following:

1. a capacity to listen to the specific language of the instructional program;
2. a reasonable span of auditory attention;
3. an accurate ear for oral language details in the specific classroom;
4. an awareness of fine visual details in the specific written language used;
5. a strong comprehension of words in spoken context;
6. a well-developed speaking vocabulary which can be used in the school setting; and
7. an organized system of spatial concepts, including directionality.

If the teaching alternative is literacy in English, then the oral language practices should certainly be in English. If, however, the native Spanish is used as a basis for Spanish print, then oral language practice should be in Spanish. Classroom practices must be consistent with the choice of language as the carrier of content and the mediator of meaning.

Cultural pressures, personal values, and individual aspirations are also influential in determining the pupil's ability to manage successfully the developmental tasks of reading and writing. The teachers of Spanish speaking pupils must examine these factors and must understand their impact on children who live in two cultural settings, often amid conflicting value systems. As development, maturation, and readiness to read are considered, the school must recognize the numerous positive attributes of Spanish speaking children: their language, their value system, and their cultural heritage. Individuals responsible for the introductory program in literacy, then, can tap these many sources of strength and use them to the pupils' advantage in the classroom. The child from a Spanish speaking home brings to school his promise and his potential for learning. The responsibility of the school is to bring to this child an educational program which takes into account his development, his maturation, his readiness, and his uniqueness.

- **Literacy Has a Speech-Print Relationship**

Reading requires a response to written forms of speech sounds. The reader must seen what has been written, he must transform what he sees into sounds, then he must associate the sounds with previous experiences recognized and remembered from his personal and real world. Through practice and success, the reader improves his ability to connect speech and print. An experienced, mature, efficient reader is able to make a direct connection between what he sees in print and what he has stored as a referent for such print. He is able to skip the intermediate step of transforming the visual symbols (print) into auditory symbols (speech). When the visual appearance of a child's language can be related (however imperfectly) to the sounds of that same language, he is usually able to make the necessary associations and to obtain meaning from them. Reading is complicated for English speaking pupils by the fact that there are discrepancies which exist between what they see and what they hear. The conventions of the English writing system dictate the representation of forty-four speech sounds by means of twenty-six written symbols. Pupils get used to seeing one written form represent many different speech elements. For example, the *ea* of br*ea*d, b*ea*d, h*ea*lth, h*ea*rth, and br*ea*k. They also learn to respond accurately to the several written forms for one speech sound, as in words like p*ay*, sl*eigh*, r*ai*n, and c*a*k*e*. They manage these irregularities because they have an oral language background of many years to help them make the correct association. Then, they must draw upon their past experiences, encoded and stored in English, in order to comprehend whatever association they have made. When Spanish speaking pupils attempt to engage in this same process, they may find it even more difficult to associate the English print they see with the Spanish speech sounds they hear. Some sounds represented in the English writing system do not exist for them at all; for example, several short vowel sounds, the consonant digraph *sh*, and many of the word endings. Further, although Spanish speaking pupils may have an abundance of information to bring to reading comprehension, these referents are encoded and stored in Spanish.

Quite often, for the Spanish speaking pupil, there are three unknowns to be managed: the unknown English print, the unfamiliar sound represented by it, and the unrecognizable referent. Developmentally, all pupils must enjoy encounters and experiences in a stimulating environment accompanied by language. They must use language to label and to store information, and they must learn the writing system of the same language in order to become efficient readers. If Spanish speaking pupils are to be successful, they must be provided with extended auditory opportunities in English so that they can become thoroughly at home in the sound system prior to an introduction to its visual appearance. They also need time to attach English labels to concepts already acquired and made meaningful in Spanish. Objects and ideas specific to the English speaking community must also be added to this store of knowledge.

There are three basic options for teachers. A first choice is to introduce the Spanish speaking child to the written forms of Spanish and to offer sequential skill development along a continuum which will promote literacy in Spanish. A second preference, the alternative which is presently most common, is to avoid any use of his native language strengths and to bring him along as rapidly as possible in English speech and print. A third alternative is to delay all English reading until oral English has been well established. All three options have a common share in the developmental nature of learning to read. They differ, however, in the purpose of the program, in the lanugage of instruction, and in the language content of the reading program itself.

- **Literacy Requires Sensorimotor Integration**

The raw material for the Spanish speaking child's perceptions of the world around him comes to him by way of his sense organs. As he receives sensory data, they are registered and made meaningful in his brain which can then organize responses as required. His earliest impressions allow him to separate himself from his environment. He discovers himself and his body. He learns the names and functions of his body parts. He acquires concepts of left and right, front and back, top and bottom. He figures out where he is in space so that he can determine where the rest of the world is in relation to his position. He has to depend upon himself and his environment in order to move and to grow. He must trust both self and surroundings in order to rely upon any information coming from either source. He must develop a preferred hand and a dominant eye as he enjoys unrestricted opportunities to use both sides of his body. The fine muscle control needed for reading and writing follows the development of gross motor skills. He must coordinate the tracking of his eye and hand to control paper and pencil demands. Like any child of language background, he must bring together the visual-motor-perceptual skills which serve as the foundation for learning to read and to write. With very minor adjustments, the existing sensorimotor programs in classrooms can be very helpful for the Spanish speaking child. For example, puzzles, manipulative materials, games, rhythms, and other lessons can be carried out by imitation and demonstration. Generally, the activities or the equipment are self-explanatory and, with very little language modification, can provide for a full range of sensorimotor improvement. An important variable is the consistency of the language which accompanies sensorimotor activities. For the pupil to trust himself and his own position in space, he must come to terms with not only spatial concepts, but also with their labels. The teacher will have to recognize pupils who have adequate awareness encoded in native language terms such as *arriba* (above), *abajo* (below), *izquierda* (left), *derecha* (right), and those who have neither concepts nor labels. During this early period, the language used can be English or Spanish depending upon the curriculum design; but, whichever the language choice, one language should be kept constant within the context of any lesson. It is confusing and detrimental for young pupils to keep switching back and forth between English and Spanish when possibly both languages are yet to be fully developed.

- **Literacy Demands Visual and Auditory Memory**

Remembering, for all children, begins with paying attention. One of the first demands the school makes upon the child is that of sustaining attention sufficient for learning. Attention requires concentration to specific stimuli presented and excludes extraneous distracting stimuli competing for the same attention. A child's attention, its duration and strength, is often a function of interest. For the Spanish speaking child, attention to visual stimuli may be distracted by the unfamiliar sounds of English with which lessons may be presented. A story accompanied by attractive pictures may capture and hold the child's attention only if the burden of listening to meaningless English accompaniment, for long periods, is avoided.

To develop visual attention and visual memory, the pupil needs practice in responding and remembering material which is relevant to the attention and memory tasks of reading. Not only does he need to be exposed to the gross visual exercises of noting detail in matching and in sequencing forms, shapes, and pictures, but he also must be given visual attention and memory activities of the actual writing system. If he is to be introduced to print by way of his second language, English, he should see and respond to *visual* patterns of English. He can note *saw/was, on/no* differences; identify all the p's in a row of p's, d's, and b's; and match pairs of words selected from English. He should receive many opportunities to find likenesses and differences among the written details of English. It is well to restate that he is reacting to these visual stimuli only in terms of their visual appearance. He is not reading them. If the decision has been made to use Spanish as the first medium for his literacy, he should match, sort, identify details, and select visually from written Spanish. Exercises such as differentiating between *la ñ* and *la n*; finding similarities in *cosa, casa, cara;* matching pairs of words, *pez luz pez*; and identifying the visual elements of the language he will later meet in reading should be offered in abundance.

All persons exhibit the phenomenon of *selective* attention; that is, they will attend longer and more intently with stimuli which is interesting and makes sense to them. Spanish speaking pupils are no different. They require repeated exposures to stimulating varieties of visual materials directly related to the reading tasks which demand strong and accurate skills in attention and memory. If any child is to remember what he has seen, then the visual material must be presented in such a way as to maximize the strength and the relevance of the visual stimuli.

When the Spanish speaking child is expected to pay attention to and remember what he has heard, then auditory materials must be presented under conditions consistent with good listening. Prior to formal reading lessons requiring the pupil to perceive and to discriminate among speech sounds, a pupil should engage in many ear training activities. Whether his ears are to be trained to listen for and to distinguish among Spanish or English sounds will depend upon the literacy program selected for him. The Spanish speaking child who is learning to read Spanish may need to have an extended period of hearing a full, rich range of Spanish as spoken by different individuals of different ages, regions, and groups. He should hear Spanish spoken by both men and women. He can benefit from listening for phonemic elements in the beginning, ending, and medial positions of words. He needs to hear the rhymes and rhythms of Spanish speech. If he is to be brought to literacy by means of second language print, activities must be provided for sound saturation and for developing the auditory abilities necessary to understand the sound system of English. The teacher has the responsibility for offering ear-training lessons in a systematic sequence and, further, has the added duty of giving nonnative pupils time for mastery of them. English speaking pupils have experienced years of language exposure in the natural, informal exchange among their families. It cannot be expected that a Spanish speaking child in the artificial setting of the classroom will internalize the sounds and structures of English in a few weeks or even months. Repetition and practice that is lively, and frequently varied, should characterize the ear-training activities. Elements of language must be overlearned if they are to be used easily and automatically by pupils. Overlearning improves memory and all pupils must develop good skills in remembering if they are to learn to read. The Spanish speaking child must overlearn the written features of English and the oral elements represented by them in order to achieve success as a reader of English. To do this, he needs patience, practice, and time.

- **Literacy Is Thought**

When any child reads in any language, he is engaging in thinking. He is remembering, associating, reasoning, judging, or interpreting. All of these actions have been described as cognitive processes. As he reads and thinks, his background of verbal material, his language, contributes greatly to the skill with which he does both. It is relatively easy for a teacher to observe reading performances of pupils, but their thinking processes are not so directly observable. Verbal symbols are among the several raw materials which are used in thinking, and language is unique to the individual and his experience in a specific linguistic community. The Spanish speaking child has a reservoir of language which serves his thought processes. If he is reading in English, however, his previously acquired Spanish language may not serve him well in thinking about what he has read. It may be of no use to him at all *or* it may seriously interfere with his comprehension of the material. The thoughts of an author can only be shared by the reader when he knows the writing system used and understands the oral language and referents for which the writing stands. The teacher must be especially alert to the comprehension problems of the Spanish speaking child, problems which may stem from the requirement to read and to think in a language which may be inadequately developed to support meaning. Language and thought relationships are not clearly understood for the monolingual child. Educators must weigh cautiously the enormous complexities existing for the child who is asked to read and to think in *two* languages. If the alternative is literacy by means of the native Spanish first, then, the verbal symbol system which is fundamental to the child's thought structure is likely to be his stronger material. Speech, print, and referent systems are consistently encoded in related symbolic substances. If he is expected to read and to think in a program of literacy in English, prudent monitoring of the reading content must be exercised to help him deal effectively with the language-thought demands of the weaker language.

- **Organizing the Reading Program**

Literacy is highly dependent upon an orderly, sequential development of skills. Like many pupils for whom English is not a native language, the Spanish speaking child may have experienced a high rate of school transfer, a concomitant disorganization of reading skills, or an inappropriate sequence of them. Each mastery of simple skills provides the basis for success with more difficult skills required later in a developmental reading program. For the child reading any language, there is an impressive array of skills which must be successfully accomplished before the more formal literacy program can be undertaken. He must learn to *decode* with speed and accuracy so that he can recognize the words and expressions on the printed page. He may be taught to do this by any number of methods or approaches. As he analyzes and recognizes written material, he must make meaning out of what he has decoded. Planned reading programs offer the skills in different sequential order. Some methods present the decoding skills basically devoid of meaning as a tool for later reading lessons more meaningful in nature. Some approaches begin with meaning first and then add the word analysis skills later. Two factors must be considered in the organization of the reading plan. The first is its consistent progression from the simple to the difficult, and the second is its suitability for the pupils who will be expected to move steadily along the skills continuum. For the Spanish speaking child, especially, as a child who is already carrying the heavy language responsibility of English and Spanish, every effort possible must be exerted to see that the literacy program of one or both languages is organized and sequenced according to a steady pace conducive to excellence.

- **Literacy Is Measurable**

Measuring the Spanish speaking pupil's literacy begins with a precise statement of what he is to do, under what conditions, and according to what standards of excellence. If he is preliterate, then, measurement begins with an estimate of his readiness to read. As stated earlier, the assessment must be made in the specific context of the literacy program to which he is to be introduced. The behaviors to be examined include oral language, body image, visual-motor control, ear training, and attention to visual detail. The teacher may observe the child's performance within each of these areas and may rate his background as strong, adequate, or weak as compared to other pupils of his age. Again, it is essential to consider the Spanish speaking pupil's readiness as assessed for either a literacy plan for native language or for second language. Obtained information gives the teacher valuable clues for where the program should begin and of what the program should consist. The data also serve to point up unusual strengths and/or special needs of the pupil which the teacher may include in the daily organization of lessons.

For example, if a child appears to have a fine background of oral language but poor sensorimotor development, his readiness program could stress activities to promote fine muscle control and visual-perceptual skills. If a child's attention to visual detail appears strong, but he has poorly developed auditory abilities, then a plan to enhance his listening habits, to extend attention span, and to increase his auditory discrimination would be most effective. Teachers are very well able to observe pupils at this stage in the reading program and to determine the most suitable lessons.

Teacher-made tests, based upon the particular reading skills presented, also serve as valuable instruments for assessing reading progress. These measures, often referred to as criterion-referenced measures, have the singular advantage of appraising pupil progress based upon the actual program of instruction. Though such tests cannot be used for determining a pupil's achievement as compared to the achievement of other pupils, they do provide useful data describing the child's growth along the skills continuum as organized for him. Teachers may also measure progress by periodic observation, structured interview, individual conferences, and other informal means.

If the Spanish speaking child is in a second-language literacy program, he is quite likely to have his reading achievement assessed by means of standardized reading tests. The language of the standardized test may be beyond his English language development; the content of the test items may be culturally unfamiliar to him; the level of the test may be too difficult in terms of his skills level in English; and the standardization sample from which the norms were derived may not have represented him in the group. Data obtained on standardized reading tests in English must be viewed cautiously. Informal reading inventories can offer teachers good information about the Spanish speaking child's ability to function independently and/or with instructional help with written English of differential degrees of difficulty.

Progress of the Spanish speaking pupil who is reading his native language may also be appraised by these same means, both formal and informal. Criterion-referenced measures of growth along the continuum of Spanish reading skills can be devised by teachers on the basis of the instructional program in Spanish. Standardized tests of Spanish reading achievement imported from Spanish speaking countries will very likely prove unsuitable because of some of the same inadequacies found in standardized tests of reading in English.

- **Standardized Tests of Reading: A Warning**

Reading achievement has always been a matter of universal concern in a world which values literacy and the literate individual. Students everywhere have been expected to advance in their quest for knowledge through the medium of a highly demanding, print-oriented curriculum. Teachers, too, have been expected to monitor students' abilities to cope successfully with materials of increasing reading difficulty. Usually, the review of student progress has taken varied forms along a continuum from informal observation by the teacher to formal assessment through the standardized test. In spite of the limitations of tests as instruments which provide adequate coverage of the many factors upon which reading proficiency depends, standardized surveys of reading abilities have continued to be the most widely used and the best known methods in school settings around the world. As data obtained on such measures serve as the basis for educational decisions, it is essential to examine the descriptive labels, *standardized* and *objective*. There are several potential hazards in using only test data in program planning under any circumstances. However, these dangers are even greater when the English reading achievement of Spanish speakers is assessed by means of testing instruments which may be both minimally objective and marginally standardized for speakers of other languages. There are several theoretical issues and some practical implications to consider.

- **Theoretical Considerations**

Measuring reading achievement of students for whom English is not a native language is an extravagant endeavor. Standardized reading tests have been administered customarily to assess *both* the levels of achievement of the students and the quality of the instructional programs. Although tests differ in kind, in efficiency, and in precision, they share the common intent of providing useful information which can be used to improve opportunities for learning. Tests have been defined as "samples of behavior," overt or symbolic. Tests have been described as "systematic procedures" for comparing the behavior of two or more persons *(1)*. Tests also purport to yield a measure of differential responses of individuals to the same stimuli. At best, all tests are thoughtful estimates and, at worst, they are dangerous guesses. In the evaluation process, of which testing is just one part, tests are merely tools. As tools, tests are as effective as the suitability of the measure used and the skill of the person using them. When the instrument selected is one that has been constructed from language and content within the perceptions of reality of a specified population (native speakers of English), its use must take into account a number of variables which may influence the outcomes and may limit considerably any inferences to be drawn from test results. The educational challenge of obtaining accurate and fair achievement data on pupils reared in different social and cultural milieux is, indeed, great.

Among the several theoretical considerations upon which the measurement of reading ability rests, there are three basic assumptions. The *first* is the assumption that the students have enjoyed equality of opportunity to have experienced an environment from which the test items have been selected. Also, implicit in this premise is the expectation of a relatively similar instructional program as well. The *second* is the assumption that there is mutual comprehensibility of the language of both the test giver and the test taker at a depth sufficient to carry out the tasks of the test, including receiving the necessary instructions and making the required responses. The *third* is the assumption that the normative data from which inferences are to be made have been gathered on a population representative of all pupils who are expected to take the test. Thus, responsible assessment of reading demands minimally that three conditions be met:

1. that the student has received comparable experiences and instruction in the content area;

2. that the student controls the verbal symbol system of English in its written form; and
3. that the student's characteristics of social class, economic status, cultural group, age, grade placement, and other essential identifying traits have been widely represented in the population sample on which the normative data have been established.

It is well appreciated that the totality of a student's ability to read is not measured in a test of an hour or two. An estimate of his reading achievement may be obtained from certain samples of reading behavior observed under certain conditions *(7)*. An objective test presumed to measure reading proficiency requires that the *same* set of circumstances apply to all students who take the test and that the test administration follow a standardized approach in matters of time, directions, assistance, and other procedural matters. Deviations or alterations of any aspect of the test administration change the outcomes and reduce the comparability of results. It is germane to ask how these theoretical questions affect the test performance of Spanish speaking students whose life experiences, native languages, and instructional programs in reading English are so different from the students for which the measures have been designed.

Of particular interest is the nature of the reading process itself. An examination of what has been tested, what has been taught, and what have been the major instructional objectives may reveal that a standardized reading test for English speaking pupils has merely measured unfamiliarity with the writing system or lack of informational background. If print exists because speech existed before it, if print owes its existence to speech, and if there is a highly interdependent relationship between speech and print, it would appear reasonable that, once the written code of English has been mastered, then students could read at a level of proficiency commensurate with their oral control of English. It cannot be assumed, however, that instructional programs in oral English only will automatically result in reading achievement. Response to print requires the student to see the visual symbols, to hear the auditory symbols which they represent, and to connect the sound-symbol associations to a meaningful referent. Written language cannot faithfully represent oral language. There are imperfections in the writing system which are problems for all who are native to English. The Spanish speaking pupil who responds to written English in terms of his own native language may experience difficulty in recognizing the sounds represented by the symbols. He may be applying the sound-symbol relationships of his native language as Spanish and English share a similar alphabet. Vocabulary items and word order, too, may be highly confusing for him. Such interference can occur as he attempts to decode English print and to make meaning of it. He may also encounter problems understanding what he has been able to decode. If the testing instrument provides different subtests for different skills and yields a vocabulary and a comprehension score, then, the data may reveal significant variables beyond the test score. If the Spanish speaking student appears to decode English print and to recognize the words as written but fails to obtain meaning from them, it is likely that his background of information encoded and stored in the English language is insufficient for effective reading. If, on the other hand, the ability to recognize words is marginal as well, then the test data may be indicative of the student's inadequately developed decoding skills. An analysis of test data should take into account the nature of his native language, both in its oral and written patterns, and the possibilities of positive and negative transfer effects. It is essential to differentiate between the reading problems of students who have excellent skills in word recognition, yet who have minimal understanding of the semantic loading, and those students who have not acquired the fundamental skills needed for unlocking unfamiliar words.

- **Practical Implications**

When students are expected to deal effectively with the writing system of English as a foreign language, teachers and administrators often face burdensome educational decisions. Many students may aspire to advance study in specialized fields of knowledge. A reasonable estimate of reading competence will assist everyone in selecting from among the available alternatives. At all levels, a test of reading English should be administered with the *purpose* for determining reading proficiency clearly in mind. Test data may be desired merely to determine the next appropriate level of reading instruction. Test information may be required to consider a nonnative speaker for admission to a college, a university, or a technical school where English is the language of instruction. Levels of reading proficiency may be needed to substantiate the advisability of technological study in areas where the essential content is published only in English. Reading competency may be a prerequisite for a governmental post in the political or diplomatic service of the country. Nonnative speaking students' interests in the social sciences and humanities may demand a broader, deeper contact with English speaking peoples of the world through their language and literature in the original. The selection and administration of tests of reading achievement must be considered on the basis of the school placement of the pupil, the nature of the information sought, the purpose for seeking it, and the decisions which the test data will influence.

If achievement data are to be of any value in the decision-making process, not only must they be directly related to the purpose for which the data were obtained, but they also must be as complete and valid as possible. Educators may find it helpful to ask some of these questions when achievement test scores for Spanish speaking pupils are reviewed.

1. Has the student enjoyed reasonable access to the experiences (either first hand or vicariously) encoded in the print of English?
2. Has the student receptive control of English at a depth sufficient to understand what he is expected to do in the test situation?
3. Does the student comprehend fully the manner in which he is to make his response?
4. Has the student expressive command of English adequate for him to answer when test items require a written or spoken response?
5. Has the student received a reasonably systematic, sequential program of instruction in speaking and reading English?
6. Have students with this student's personal, social, and cultural characteristics been included in the normative data?

If most of these questions cannot be answered in the affirmative, then, any inferences relative to the student's performance must be made very tentatively and the obtained data must be used very cautiously. It is most likely that the data represent only present performance narrowly circumscribed within the many sources of error previously mentioned. The data have minimal value for *classifying* the sum total of the student's ability to read English. It is certainly possible that other measures, other fields of knowledge, other cultural and social content, other time constraints within the same or comparable level of difficulty could provide different outcomes.

The data may have *predictive* value. They may predict future reading performance in academic settings where reading English is essential to survival. Useful information may be gathered if the examiner wishes to go beyond the score as a quantified classification. An analysis of the student's test performance on individual test items provides insights into specific reading requirements which were handled successfully and those which were a source of error. Each response may provide clues regarding the student's ability to persist, to reason verbally, and to solve problems presented in the print of another language. Such information can be used to document the student's reading strengths, to diagnose his special reading needs, to identify the kinds of materials he can read independently, and to serve as the basis for future educational decisions. Careful examination beyond the single, numerical score makes judgments possible beyond the classification level which may, in some instances, result in arbitrary selection of students for placement or advancement purposes. Teachers and administrators may have a better basis for making fair and equitable decisions regarding their Spanish speaking students. It would be blatantly unjust to deny students the opportunities they may seek when the test data upon which the choice was made may be highly questionable.

In summary, the appraisal of reading achievement in English as a foreign language is a difficult and demanding challenge to educators everywhere. Standardized reading tests normed on a population of native speakers of English provide only limited estimates of reading achievement and potential of students for whom English is a foreign language. It seems prudent to caution users of standardized measures of the several sources of variability and of error in these instruments when they are used with students who have been reared in different social, cultural, economic, and educational settings. Test selection must be made on the basis of the specific purpose for testing. Further analyses of test results beyond the total and/or subtest scores provide useful diagnostic information. There are many risks involved in appraising the reading achievement of students for whom English is a foreign language. To make wise educational decisions for students, educators must be well aware of the number and kind of hazards involved in the use of standardized tests. It is prudent to augment obtained test data with all other information available. Teacher-made tests developed for assessing specific skill acquisition may not offer a basis for comparing a student's performance with a group. However, such criterion-referenced measures devised to measure specific reading areas will give reasonable estimates of how a student functions along the reading skills continuum. Informal reading inventories are useful for determining the level of difficulty a student can manage without failure and frustration. A teacher's sensitive ear in oral reading sessions or in class discussions of material read silently can serve as a precision instrument to check comprehension. The means by which a student's reading potential and achievement can be evaluated are multiple. Teachers and administrators should be encouraged to use any and all methods best suited to obtain the most accurate and most predictive estimate of reading achievement for *all* students, but especially for those who are reading in a language not native to them.

Yet, teachers of reading in Spanish have the need to determine progress rates and to decide whether their pupils are moving along at a pace commensurate with readers of English. There are few, if any, tests of reading which meet the rigorous criteria of validity and reliability for use with a population of Spanish speaking pupils who are moving back and forth between two languages and two cultural influences. Until adequate measures of reading achievement in Spanish can be developed and researched, the levels of accomplishment of these pupils can be determined by other means. One technique is the assigning of a reading difficulty index to the materials available for use in the Spanish reading classroom. An index based upon the sentence lengths, word frequency, and/or the number of polysyllabic words and other indicators of reading complexity may be applied. The work of

Spaulding *(5, 6)* and Patterson *(4)* would be most helpful for educators who should wish to analyze the readability of the Spanish literacy program materials. Of course, an analysis of Spanish written materials should be undertaken only by persons with native or near-native skills in the Spanish language. After an identification of the levels of reading difficulty, teachers could then group books and worksheets into units of comparable readability and arrange them in a hierarchy from the easy to the difficult in such a manner as to support steady, continuing progress. Still another method of measuring reading achievement for the Spanish speaking child could be accomplished by assigning English equivalent grade level designations to comparable stages in the Spanish reading program. A committee of teachers familiar with the expected performances of pupils from the preprimer through the sixth grade readers could examine the skills and contents at each specific level for each language and could come to some concensus regarding anticipated achievement. There are numerous reading skills common to successful achievement in both languages and there are some unique requirements for each language. Through a thorough and thoughtful examination of both of the reading programs, the group could identify equivalent levels of achievement and develop a useful yardstick by which to judge the progress of the Spanish speaking reader of Spanish. Measurement should be a *part* of the process by which the literacy program is evaluated. It should serve the purpose of evaluation by providing data upon which the reading plans can be redirected as needed to better serve children. The school has a serious responsibility for avoiding measurement techniques which may be unreasonable, unproductive, and damaging to the self-confidence of any child, especially one who needs to feel accepted, respected, and successful in a culturally different setting.

- **An Index of Reading Difficulty**

It is feasible to assess reading levels or to estimate reading achievement gains by means of a careful appraisal of the actual material the pupil is able to read and to understand. The readability of classroom materials is often a function of interest *and* of language difficulty. While the interest factor is highly personal and specific to individuals or groups, the characteristics of sentence length, common word usage, and structural complexity can be identified. Easy materials are written in familiar vocabularies, short sentences, and simple structures. Difficult materials consist of long, involved sentences arranged in complex structures which contain unfamiliar words. As the pupil demonstrates his ability as a reader to cope with material which increases in its level of difficulty according to these specific criteria, the teacher can determine the extent of his progress.

Seth Spaulding *(5, 6)* and Frank Patterson *(4)* have provided formulas for determining the relative level of difficulty of Spanish written materials to obtain an *index of readability;* they recommend the following procedure.

List I     For the selection of a sample of content:
1. *In long selections*
   a. Analyze samples of 100 words every ten pages.
2. *In shorter selections*
   b. Analyze samples of 500 words every 1,000 words.
3. *In selections of 500 words or fewer*
   c. Analyze the entire passage.

List II     To apply the formula:
1. Count the number of words in the sample.
2. Count the number of sentences.
3. Divide the number of words by the number of sentences. Result is average sentence length.
4. Check the words against List I and count the number of words not in the list.
5. Divide the number of words not on the list by the number of words in the sample. The result is the density or complexity of the vocabulary.
6. Using the table, find the number which corresponds to the density.
7. Find the number which corresponds to the average sentence length.
8. Draw a line to connect the two points of density and average sentence length.
9. The point at which the two lines intersect the central column represents the relative difficulty of the sample.

    According to Patterson, an index above 80 indicates that the material is moving toward a level of reading difficulty which may make the material more obscure to readers of limited education. An index of 100 suggests very difficult reading, and one of over 120 is indicative of a high degree of reading difficulty.

    The levels of difficulty and the grades at which materials should be presented are suggested as reasonable and approximate. Pupils with well-developed language backgrounds or with previous instructional opportunities may be moved along the continuum at a more rapid pace. Pupils who need more exposure and time for the acquisition of skills may be provided with additional review and/or entry at a more basic level. Spaulding was interested in analyzing written Spanish for readers who were *not* native to the language so his formula may be viewed tentatively for *native* Spanish speakers. Patterson was interested in writing for *native* Spanish speakers. Both researchers used sentence length and common word usage as features in their estimates of reading difficulty. Though there is great need to investigate the applicability of their work to pupils in the elementary school, their ideas do represent a reasonable alternative to use and misuse of inappropriate testing instruments.

The *Index of Reading Difficulty* ranges from 20 to 160 and can be divided as follows:

20–40 Primer level
40–60 Very easy

60–80 Easy

80–100 Relatively Easy
100–120 Difficult
120–160 Very difficult

40—Grade 1
50—Grade 2
60—Grade 3
60—Grade 4
70—Grade 5
80—Grade 6
Grades 6–7–8
Grades 8–10
Grades 11–12 and above

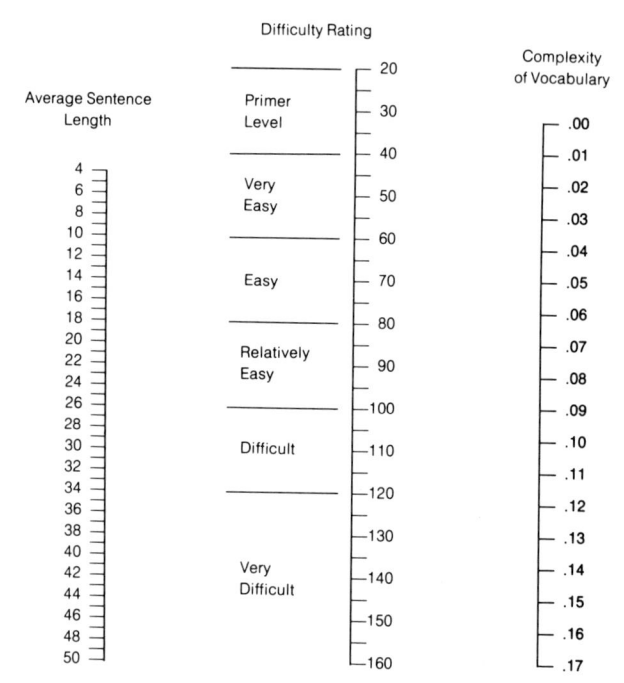

**Figure 1.** Readability Graph

Reprinted from Seth Spaulding, "A Spanish Readability Formula," *Modern Language Journal,* 40 (December 1956), 435.

# BUCHANAN AND RODRIGUEZ-BOU WORD LIST
## List I

| | | | | |
|---|---|---|---|---|
| a | ahogar | año | ave | cabeza |
| abajo | ahora | apagar | aventura | cabo |
| abandonar | aire | aparecer | avisar | cada |
| aborrecer | ajeno | apartar | ay | cadena |
| abrazar | al | aparte | ayer | caer |
| abrir | ala | apenas | ayudar | café |
| absoluto | alcalde | aplicar | azúcar | caída |
| abuelo | alcanzar | apoyar | azul | caja |
| acá | alegrar | aprender | | c(u)alidad |
| acabar | alegre | apretar | bailar | calma |
| acaso | alegría | aprovechar | bajar | calor |
| acción | alejar | aquel, | bajo | callar |
| aceite | algo | aquél | balcón | calle |
| acento | alguien | aquí | bañar | cama |
| aceptar | algún (-o) | árbol | barba | cambiar |
| acerca | aliento | arder | base | cambio |
| acercar | alma | ardiente | bastante | caminar |
| acertar | alrededor | arma | bastar | camino |
| acompañar | alterar | armar | batalla | campana |
| aconsejar | alto | arrancar | batir | campaña |
| acordar | altura | arrastrar | beber | campo |
| acostumbrar | alumbrar | arreglar | belleza | cansar |
| actitud | alzar | arriba | bello | cantar |
| acto | allá | arrojar | bendecir | cantidad |
| actual | allí | arte | bendito | canto |
| acudir | amable | artículo | besar | capa |
| acuerdo | amante | artista | beso | capaz |
| adelantar | amar | asegurar | bestia | capital |
| adelante | amargo | así | bien (s., | capitán |
| ademas | amargura | asiento | adv.)* | capítulo |
| adiós | ambos | asistir | blanco | cara |
| admirable | amenazar | asomar | blando | carácter |
| admiración | americano | asombrar | boca | cárcel |
| admirar | amigo | aspecto | boda | cargar |
| admitir | amistad | aspirar | bondad | cargo |
| adonde | amo | asunto | bonito (adj.) | caridad |
| adorar | amor | atar | bosque | cariño |
| adquirir | amoroso | atencion | bravo | carne |
| advertir | anciano | atender | brazo | carrera |
| afán | ancho | atento | breve | carro |
| afecto | andar | atrás | brillante | carta |
| afirmar | ángel | atrevesar | brillar | casa |
| afligir | angustia | atreverse | buen (-o) | casar |
| agitar | animal | aumentar | burla | casi |
| agradable | animar | aun, aún | burlar | caso |
| agradar | animo | aunque | buscar | castellano |
| agradecer | anterior | ausencia | | castigar |
| agregar | antes | autor | caballero | castigo |
| agua | antiguo | autoridad | caballo | causa |
| aguardar | anunciar | auxilio | cabello | causar |
| ahí | añadir | avanzar | caber | ceder |

*s. = substantivo (noun); adv. = adverbio; adj. = adjetivo; v. = verbo; prep. = preposición; pron. = pronombre.

55

| | | | | |
|---|---|---|---|---|
| celebrar | condición | costa | delicado | distinguir |
| célebre | conducir | costar | demás | distinto |
| centro | conducta | costumbre | demasiado | diverso |
| ceñir | confesar | crear | demonio | divertir |
| cerca | confianza | crecer | demonstrar | dividir |
| cercano | confiar | creer | dentro | divino |
| cerebro | conforme | criado | derecho (-a) | doblar |
| cerrar | confundir | criar | derramar | doble |
| cesar | confusion | criatura | desaparecer | doctor |
| ciego | confuso | cristal | descansar | dolor |
| cielo | conjunto | cristiano | descanso | dominar |
| ciencia | conmigo | cruel | desconocer | don, D. |
| cierto (-a- | conmover | cruz | describir | donde, dónde |
| mente) | conocer | cruzar | descubrir | doña, Da. |
| circunstancia | conocimiento | cuadro | desde | dormir |
| citar | conque | cual, cuál | desear | drama |
| ciudad | conquista | cualquiera | deseo | duda |
| civil | consagrar | cuando, | desesperar | dudar |
| claridad | consecuencia | cuándo | desgracia | dueño |
| claro | conseguir | cuanto, cuánto | desgraciado | dulce |
| clase | consejo | cuarto (s.) | deshacer | dulzura |
| clavar | consentir | cubrir | desierto | durante |
| cobrar | conservar | cuello | despedir | durar |
| cocer | considerar | cuenta | despertar | duro |
| coche | consigo | cuento | despreciar | |
| coger | consistir | cuerpo | después | e |
| cólera | constante | cuestión | destinar | echar |
| colgar | constituir | cuidado | destino | edad |
| colocar | construir | cuidar | destruir | edificio |
| color | consuelo | culpa | detener | educación |
| columna | consumir | culto | determinar | efecto |
| combatir | contar | cumbre | detrás | ejecutar |
| comedia | contemplar | cumplir | día | ejemplo |
| comenzar | contener | cura | diablo | ejercer |
| comer | contento | curiosidad | diario | ejército |
| cometer | contestar | curioso | dicha | el, el |
| comida | contigo | curso | dicho (s.) | elegir |
| como, cómo | continuar | chico | dichoso | elemento |
| compañero | continuo | | diente | elevar |
| compañia | contra | dama | diferencia | ella |
| comparar | contrario | daño | diferente | emoción |
| complacer | contribuir | dar | difícil | empeñar |
| completo | convencer | de | dificultad | empezar |
| componer | convenir | debajo | difunto | emplear |
| comprar | conversación | deber (v.o s.) | digno | emprender |
| comprender | convertir | débil | dinero | empresa |
| común | convidar | decidir | dios | en |
| comunicar | copa | decir | direccion | enamorar |
| con | corazón | declarar | directo | encantador |
| concebir | corona | dedicar | dirigir | encanto |
| conceder | correr | dedo | discreto | encargar |
| concepto | corresponder | defecto | discurrir | encender |
| conciencia | corriente | defender | discurso | encerrar |
| concluir | cortar | defensa | disgusto | encima |
| conde | corte | dejar | disponer | encontrar |
| condenar | corto | del | disposicion | encuentro |
| condesa | cosa | delante | distancia | enemigo |

| | | | | |
|---|---|---|---|---|
| energía | estudiar | formar | habitacion | imitar |
| enfermedad | estudio | formidable | habitar | impedir |
| enfermo | eterno | fortuna | hablar | imperio |
| engañar | evitar | frances | hacer | imponer |
| engaño | exacto | franco | hacia | importancia |
| enojo | examinar | frase | hacienda | importante |
| enorme | excelente | frecuente | hallar | importar |
| enseñanza | exclamar | frente | hambre | imposible |
| enseñar | exigir | fresco | harto | impresión |
| entender | existencia | frío | hasta | impreso |
| enterar | existir | fruto | he aquí | imprimir |
| entero | experiencia | fuego | hecho (s.) | impulse |
| entonces | experimentar | fuente | helar | inclinar |
| entrada | explicar | fuera | herida | indicar |
| entrar | exponer | fuerte | herir | indiferente |
| entre | expresar | fuerza | hermano | individuo |
| entregar | expresión | función | hermoso | industria |
| entusiasmo | extender | fundar | hermosura | infeliz |
| enviar | extensión | futuro | hervir | infierno |
| envolver | extranjero | | hierro | infinito |
| época | extrañar | galán | hijo | influencia |
| error | extraño | gana | hilo | ingenio |
| escapar | extraordinario | ganar | historia | inglés |
| escaso | extremo | gastar | hogar | inmediato |
| escena | | gato | hoja | inmenso |
| escalvo | facil | general | hombre | inocente |
| escoger | facultad | género | hombro | inquieto |
| esconder | falda | generoso | hondo | inspirar |
| escribir | falso | genio | honor | instante |
| escritor | falta | gente | honra | instrumento |
| escuchar | fama | gesto | honrar | inteligencia |
| escuela | familia | gitano | hora | intención |
| ese, ése | famoso | gloria | horrible | intentar |
| esfuerzo | fantasía | glorioso | horror | interés |
| eso | favor | gobernar | hoy | interesante |
| espacio | favorecer | gobierno | huerta | interesar |
| espada | fe | golpe | hueso | interior |
| espalda | felicidad | gota | huevo | interrumpir |
| español | feliz | gozar | huir | íntimo |
| esparcir | fenómeno | gracia | humanidad | introducir |
| especial | feo | gracioso | humano | inútil |
| especie | fiar | grado | humilde | invierno |
| espejo | fiel | gran (-de) | humo | ir (-se) |
| esperanza | fiesta | grandeza | hundir | ira |
| esperar | figura | grave | | isla |
| espeso | figurar | griego | idea | izquierdo |
| espíritu | fijar | gritar | ideal | |
| esposo | fijo | grito | idioma | jamás |
| establecer | fin | grupo | iglesia | jardín |
| estado | final | guapo | ignorar | jefe |
| estar | fingir | guardar | igual | joven |
| estatua | fino | guerra | iluminar | juego |
| este, éste | firme | guiar | ilusión | juez |
| estilo | físico | gustar | ilustre | jugar |
| estimar | flor | gusto | imagen | juicio |
| estrecho | fondo | | imaginación | juntar |
| estrella | forma | haber | imaginar | junto |

57

| | | | | |
|---|---|---|---|---|
| jurar | llegar | mío | nombre | página |
| justicia | llenar | mirada | norte | país |
| justo | lleno | mirar (v.) | nota | pájaro |
| juventud | llevar | misa | notable | palabra |
| juzgar | llorar | miserable | notar | palacio |
| | | miseria | noticia | pan |
| la | madre | mismo | novio | papel |
| labio | maestro | misterio | nube | par |
| labor | magnífico | misterioso | nuevo | para |
| labrador | majestad | mitad | número | parar |
| lado | mal (-o) (adj., | moderno | numeroso | parecer (v.) |
| ladrón | s. o adv.) | modesto | nunca | pared |
| lágrima | mandar | modo | | parte |
| lance | manera | molestar | o | particular |
| lanzar | manifestar | momento | obedecer | partida |
| largo | mano | montaña | objeto | partido |
| lástima | mantener | montar | obligación | partir |
| lavar | mañana | monte | obligar | pasado |
| lazo | máquina | moral | obra | pasar |
| lector | mar | morir | obscuridad | pasear |
| lecho | maravilla | mortal | obscuro | paseo |
| leer | marcar | mostrar | observación | pasión |
| legua | marchar | motivo | observer | paso |
| lejano | marido | mover | obtener | patria |
| lejos | mas, más | movimiento | ocasión | paz |
| lengua | masa | mozo | ocultar | pecado |
| lento | matar | muchacho | oculto | pecho |
| letra | materia | mucho | ocupacion | pedazo |
| levantar | material | mudar | ocupar | pedir |
| leve | matrimonio | muerte | ocurrir | pegar |
| ley | mayor | mujer | odio | peligro |
| libertad | me | mundo | ofender | peligroso |
| librar | médico | murmurar | oficial | pelo |
| libre | medida | música | oficio | pena |
| libro | medio | muy | ofrecer | penetrar |
| ligero | medir | | oído | pensamiento |
| limitar | mejor | nacer | oír | pensar |
| límite | mejorar | nación | ojo | peor |
| limpio | memoria | nacional | olor | pequeño |
| lindo | menester | nada | olvidar | perder |
| línea | menos | nadie | opinión | perdón |
| líquido | mentir | natural | oponer | perdonar |
| lo | mentira | naturaleza | oración | perfecto |
| loco | menudo | necesario | orden | periódico |
| locura | merced | necesidad | ordenar | permanecer |
| lograr | merecer | necesitar | ordinario | permitir |
| lucha | mérito | necio | oreja | pero |
| luchar | mes | negar | orgullo | perro |
| luego | mesa | negocio | origen | perseguir |
| lugar | meter | negro | orilla | persona |
| luna | mezcla | ni | oro | personaje |
| luz | mi, mí | ninguno | otro | personal |
| llama | miedo | niño | | pertenecer |
| llamar | mientras | no | paciencia | pesar (v. o s.) |
| llano | militar | noble | padecer | peseta |
| llanto | ministro | noche | padre | peso |
| llave | minuto | nombrar | pagar | picar |

| | | | | |
|---|---|---|---|---|
| pico | proceder | recorrer | rojo | serio |
| pie | procurar | recuerdo | romper | servicio |
| piedad | producir | reducir | ropa | servir |
| piedra | profundo | referir | rosa | severo |
| piel | prometer | regalar | rostro | si, sí |
| pieza | pronto | region | rubio | siempre |
| pintar | pronunciar | regla | rueda | siglo |
| pisar | propiedad | reina | ruido | significar |
| placer | propio | reinar | ruina | siguiente |
| planta | propener | reino | rumor | silencio |
| plata | proporcion | reír | | silla |
| plato | proporcionar | relación | saber (v.) | simple |
| plaza | propósito | relativo | sabio | sin |
| pluma | proseguir | religión | sacar | sin embargo |
| población | protestar | religioso | sacerdote | sincero |
| pobre | provincia | remedio | sacrificio | singular |
| poco | próximo | remoto | sacudir | sino |
| poder (v. o s.) | prueba | rendir | sagrado | siquiera |
| poderoso | publicar | reñir | sal | sistema |
| poeta | público | reparar | sala | sitio |
| política | pueblo | repartir | salida | situación |
| político | puerta | repetir | salir | situar |
| polvo | puerto | replicar | saltar | soberano |
| poner | pues | reposar | salud | soberbio |
| poquito | punta | reposo | saludar | sobre (prep.) |
| por | punto | representar | salvar | sobrino |
| porque, | puro | república | sangre | social |
|   porqué | | resistir | sano | sociedad |
| porvenir | que, qué | resolución | santo | sol |
| poseer | quedar (-se) | resolver | satisfacer | soldado |
| posesión | queja | respe(c)tar | satisfecho | soledad |
| posible | quejarse | respe(c)to | se | soler |
| posición | quemar | respirar | seco | solicitar |
| precio | querer | responder | secreto | solo, sólo |
| precioso | querido | respuesta | seguida | soltar |
| preciso | quien, quién | resto | seguir | sombra |
| preferir | quienquiera | resultado | según | sombrero |
| pregunta | quitar | resultar | segundo | someter |
| preguntar | quizá, quizás | retirar | seguridad | sonar |
| premio | | retrato | seguro | sonido |
| prenda | rama | reunión | semana | sonreír |
| prender | rapido | reunir | semejante | soñar |
| preparar | raro | revolver | sencillo | sordo |
| presencia | rato | rey | seno | sorprender |
| presentar | rayo | rico | sensación | sorpresa |
| presente | raza | ridículo | sentar | sospechar |
| presidente | razón | riesgo | sentido (s.) | sostener |
| prestar | real | rigor | sentimiento | suave |
| pretender | realidad | rincón | sentir | subir |
| primero | realizar | río | seña | suceder |
| primo | recibir | riqueza | señal | suceso |
| principal | recién | risa | señalar | suelo |
| príncipe | reciente | robar | señor (-a) | suelto |
| principio | reclamar | rodar | señorito (-a) | sueño |
| prisa | recoger | rodear | separar | suerte |
| privar | reconocer | rodilla | ser (v. o s.) | suficiente |
| probar | recordar | rogar | sereno | sufrir |

59

| | | | | | |
|---|---|---|---|---|---|
| sujeto | tener | trabajo | valiente | vez |
| suma | terminar | traer | valor | viaje |
| sumo | termino | traje | valle | vicio |
| superior | terreno | tranquilo | vanidad | víctima |
| suplicar | terrible | tras | vano | vida |
| suponer | terror | trasladar | vapor | viejo |
| supremo | tesoro | tratar | variar | viento |
| supuesto | testigo | trato | vario | vino |
| suspender | ti | través | varón | violencia |
| suspirar | tiempo | triste | vaso | violento |
| | tienda | tristeza | vecino | virgen |
| tabla | tierno | triunfar | vela | virtud |
| tal | tierra | triunfo | velar | visión |
| tal vez | tío | tropezar | vencer | visita |
| talento | tipo | tu, tú | vender | visitar |
| también | tirano | turbar | venganza | vista |
| tampoco | tirar | | venir | visto |
| tan | título | u | venta | viudo |
| tanto | tocar | último | ventana | vivir |
| tardar | todavía | un, uno (-a) | ventura | vivo |
| tarde (adv. | todo | único | ver | volar |
| o s.) | tomar | unión | verano | voluntad |
| te (pron.) | tono | unir | veras | volver |
| teatro | tonto | usar | verbo | voto |
| tema | torcer | uso | verdad | voz |
| temblar | tornar | usted | verdadero | vuelta |
| temer | torno | útil | verde | |
| temor | toro | | vergüenza | y |
| templo | torre | vacío | verso | ya |
| temprano | total | vago | vestido | yo |
| tender | trabajar | valer | vestir | |

- **Literacy and Two Language Systems**

There is no question that the Spanish speaking child must ultimately possess the best possible skills in comprehending, speaking, reading, and writing English regardless of the language or method selected from the available alternatives. It may be that the school's decision is to provide only monolingual experiences entirely in English and to expect that any maintenance of Spanish will be carried on by the home. Under these circumstances, the language curriculum, including the reading dimension, will proceed along a modified plan designed to offer the best chances for success for the Spanish speaking child. On the other hand, if it is decided that the pupil enter literacy by way of his native language, there remains still the requirement of offering him an appropriate sequence of English language skills. Many unresolved issues exist regarding the time to add written English to the instructional program. How to transfer native language skills to English and how to prevent interference from them are also vital matters in planning for sequential development.

A plan of literacy which will promote the ability to read both English and Spanish should begin, as do all good plans, with the learner, himself, and should be organized according to the best principles of learning as they apply to his uniqueness. A few general recommendations may be offered to guide the structuring of a dual language curriculum. Specific strategies and materials should be selected on the basis of more intimate knowledge of the Spanish speaking pupil for whom the program is intended. A few suggestions follow:

1. There should be continuing opportunities for encounters with a stimulating environment so that concepts may be acquired and clarified.
2. Such experiences should be accompanied by Spanish if the pupils are very young and/or if the experiences serve to promote totally new concepts.
3. Pupils should receive daily, systematic instruction in oral Spanish to enhance their proficiencies in the sound, structural, lexical, and semantic systems of their native language.
4. Prereading, basic reading, and advanced reading skills in Spanish should be provided according to an organized scope and sequence of Spanish.
5. Pupils should be proffered access to the fields of knowledge, to mathematics, science, social science, and other subjects, by way of the print which they control.
6. English should be given on an oral basis only while the native language strengths in literacy are in the introductory stage.
7. English-as-a-second-language, as an oral program, should be a substantial, important dimension of the curriculum.
8. English language activities should be active, interesting, varied, and delightful in content.
9. Readiness to read English should be carefully appraised after the code of the Spanish writing system has been overlearned.
10. Transfer possibilities from native language literacy should be identified and capitalized upon.

*The best predictor of success in a second language is success in the first language.* Pupils who have mastered the print of Spanish have many abilities which transfer positively to the reading of English. Both languages share the same alphabetic principle and have common roots in the Roman alphabet. Spanish and English both are ordered in a left-to-right sequence. Both have many cognates in the written and spoken forms. Literate Spanish speaking pupils can transfer appreciation of these characteristics to the task of reading English. They can, with good teaching, manage to read and to write the two languages which press upon them from their home and their school environments. They can realize their full potential for becoming bilingual, bicultural, and biliterate citizens.

- **Unresolved Issues**

One of the major issues is the question of an *immersion* versus a *second language* approach. Under an *immersion* plan, the pupil acquires the new language in a natural classroom setting within whatever content area that is being presented. Thus, an English speaking pupil in a Spanish immersion program would be given mathematics, science, social science, and other subjects in Spanish. He would receive pictorial support, demonstrations, manipulative materials, and other nonverbal clues to support his comprehension. At no time, however, would his native English be used to translate or to mediate meaning. This approach is one that has been offered for over a century to immigrants in schools of the United States. Speakers of other languages have been immersed in English and have been expected to acquire the content of the curriculum and the language which carries the content at the same time.

A *second language* approach is one which emphasizes the structure and vocabulary of the language itself and is presented separately from the content areas. Instruction is arranged according to a specific scope and sequence of language skills. The second language lessons are organized to provide optimum practice with units of language. Pupils are taught to use mimicry and memorization and to repeat utterances until they have become automatic responses. Most of the programs designed to serve Spanish speaking pupils use the second-language approach. There are some minor variations in the practical implementation of both approaches depending upon time, resources, materials, and other factors. The place of the reading program and its characteristics would, of course, be different for an immersion and for a second language approach.

One debate which frequently occurs among teachers of Spanish reading concerns the values of a *visual* or an *auditory* emphasis. Proponents of an auditory approach argue that the regular sound-symbol correspondences in the Spanish writing system make it easier for pupils to learn the speech-print relationships. They state, further, that pupils' decoding skills rapidly become powerful instruments for unlocking new, unfamiliar words. They cite the sense of confidence which pupils bring to print once they have acquired the basic rules for understanding written Spanish. Advocates of a visual approach on the other hand, feel that whole words or groups of words are more meaningful to the pupils and that undue emphasis on decoding symbols and syllables may result in dull, repetitive lessons unrelated to pupils' interests. They stress the richness and naturalness of language unhampered by the restrictions of a set of rules. Like many controversies over the relative merits of methods, the answers depend upon the differences in teachers and in their pupils. Since the whole concept of teaching Spanish reading in schools of the United States is fairly new and untried, questions of the worth of these and other approaches are still unanswered.

In many school communities the issue of the *teacher* of the Spanish reading class is a sensitive one. Should the teacher be a native Spanish speaker? If not a native speaker, then how much competence in Spanish should the teacher be expected to have? What specific training for teaching Spanish reading is necessary? Where does the teacher who has been trained to teach English-as-a-second-language to Spanish speaking pupils fit in the reading program? How do paraprofessionals who are native Spanish speakers but are untrained as teachers contribute best to the instructional plan? These are but a few of the many concerns relative to the selection and assignment of teachers.

One of the most frequently debated issues is that of transition into the English reading program. In programs which are presently being offered, there appear to be three major variations. One view is that Spanish speaking pupils should receive reading instruction only in Spanish until such time as they have mastered and consolidated the basic skills of reading in their native language. Then, they may be exposed to English print commensurate with their oral backgrounds in English. Another view is that Spanish speaking pupils should receive simultaneous instruction in reading Spanish and English as they move through the bilingual curriculum. Thus, they learn two oral and two written systems at the same time. The third viewpoint is that Spanish speaking pupils can begin to read in Spanish and when they have minimal English skills on an oral basis, they can begin to read in English. Though they are reading in two languages, the second language reading program moves more slowly and lags considerably behind the reading program in the native language. There is a need for careful research to determine which plan provides the best benefits for pupils.

There are many issues of funding, of teacher certification, of community acceptance, of staff development, and of legal responsibilities. There is a lack of solid information to resolve dilemmas concerning literacy for Spanish speaking pupils in schools of the United States. As yet, bilingual education is imprecisely defined and poorly understood among monolingual educators and administrators. The state of the art is still very primitive and crude, especially in such areas as determining language dominance, organizing dual language curricula, and evaluating the effectiveness of bilingual programs. Though there are centuries of reading research in English to draw upon, there are few studies of Spanish reading in English speaking countries. The general issues mentioned and many more will and should be debated thoughtfully as educators make greater efforts to offer more reasonable and relevant reading programs to pupils who speak Spanish.

Chapter 4

## LITERACY PUTS IT ALL TOGETHER

- **The Child**

In discussing the Spanish speaking child and his success in reading, the primary consideration is that he is a child with the same range of developmental needs shared by all children of his age, anywhere. His success or failure is likely to be dictated by the demands made on him by the school and by the kind of reading program offered him. His own oral language proficiency in Spanish or in English determines to a great extent the most appropriate approach to literacy for him. Pupils at the preliterate stage of language acquisition, those who are literate in Spanish, and those who are functionally illiterate need differentially paced reading programs which are organized on the basis of a careful assessment of language background, social-cultural variables, and personal needs. It seems prudent to remember that success in reading for the Spanish speaking child, no more or no less than for the child from any language group, is for *him* a function of good materials; suitable methods; appropriate pacing; careful, ongoing assessment; *and* a competent, caring teacher.

- **The Alternative Selected**

The decision to offer native language literacy for the Spanish speaking child or to bring him into a reading program in the second language, English, is a difficult choice complicated by community preferences, educational resources, and political exigencies. Either course of action will require a thoughtful assessment of methods of teaching reading in English or in Spanish so that approaches which are best suited for the child can be selected. Of critical concern is the question of sequencing and pacing the lessons according to the capacity of the learner to benefit from them. There are many logical and philosophical reasons for choosing native language literacy as the introductory program, but there are also many economic and social reasons for hastening the Spanish speaking child's entrance into English print. The dilemma of choice must be resolved according to the special circumstances of time, place, and conditions of the educational setting in which the child is found.

The responsibility of selecting the alternative is rarely that of the teacher alone. The community through its school board and its superintendent may express a preference for a plan of instruction which will maintain the native Spanish language. Parents of Spanish-speaking pupils often have mixed feelings about a program of Spanish reading. They are eager for their children to acquire the English language skills which will permit them to compete and to cope with the demands of school and society. They may feel that their own language inadequacies have kept them out of better employment. They want the best for their children. At the same time, parents do appreciate the acceptance and respect given their native Spanish. Further, they enjoy the many opportunities for sharing in their children's school work when it is accomplished in the language of the home. Administrators, too, may influence the choice based upon their resources of personnel, materials, funds, and personal expertise in supervising a dual language curriculum. All individuals who are to be affected by the program selection should be involved in the decision-making process. A few questions to guide the decision follow:

1. Does the community have use for Spanish in stores, banks, public buildings?
2. Are there employment opportunities for Spanish-English speakers?
3. Does the school board understand the rationale and philosophy which supports the use of Spanish as one of the languages of instruction?
4. Do parents approve of the instructional goals and objectives as stated for *both* languages?
5. Are there resources—money, materials, and personnel—available to support the plan?
6. Will the administrators offer assistance and leadership necessary for success?
7. Are teachers in other areas of the curriculum informed and accepting of the challenge the alternatives represent?
8. Do pupils show interest and enthusiasm for improving their native language as well as for acquiring a second one?

The list of questions could be lengthened as each school and community group would have to consider the options as they apply.

- **The Program**

Regardless of the literacy goal—Spanish or English—the reading program must consider *both* the developmental nature of literacy and the developmental nature of the child. The place of reading and writing tasks must be in harmony with the timetable of the child's own growth;

and, for most children, literacy is the developmental task of middle childhood, the period between ages six and ten years. The reading program should be based upon a full awareness of speech-print relationships and should insure that speech precedes the print which represents it and owes its existence to it. Literacy also consists of highly demanding neurological tasks which require an integration of sensorimotor skills. Prereading activities for all children reading any language must take these requirements into account. Learning to read and to write involves attention, memory, perception, and cognition which must be nurtured through an organized sequential program of skill development. The progress of the Spanish speaking child must be monitored along the way and program changes must be made as indicated. The school is an institution of society, created primarily for the purpose of providing literacy to all the students it serves. Pupils who can read and write effectively enlarge their horizons and change the world. Literacy is the great gift of the school. It must not be denied *any* pupil who comes to the classroom. Literacy cannot be allowed to slip from the grasp of the Spanish speaking child because his language, culture, and heritage may be different. The ability to read and to write well in at least one language should be the ultimate end-in-view for everyone; for the Spanish speaking child, the goal could be the ability to read and write two languages, the native language of his cherished home and the second language of his beloved country.

**References**

1. Chronbach, Lee J. *Essentials of Psychological Testing.* New York: Harper Brothers, 1960.
2. Garcia, Ricardo L. "Mexican-Americans Learn through Language Experience," *Reading Teacher,* 28 (December 1974), 301–305.
3. Havighurst, Robert. *Developmental Tasks and Education.* New York: Longmans Green, 1953.
4. Patterson, Frank. *Como escribir para ser entendido.* El Paso, Texas: Casa Bautista de Publicaciones, 1972.
5. Spaulding, Seth. "A Spanish Readability Formula," *Modern Language Journal,* 40 (December 1956), 433–441.
6. Spaulding, Seth. "Two Formulas for Estimating the Reading Difficulty of Spanish," *Educational Research Bulletin,* 30 (May 16, 1951), 117–124.
7. Strang, Ruth. *Diagnostic Teaching and Reading.* New York: McGraw-Hill, 1964.
8. Thonis, Eleanor W. *Teaching Reading to Non-English Speakers.* New York: Collier Macmillan International, 1970.

## Additional Suggested Readings

1. Andersson, Theodore, and Mildred Boyer. *Bilingual Schooling in the United States.* Austin, Texas: Southwest Educational Development Laboratory, 1970. Available from U. S. Government Printing Office, Washington, D. C. 20402.
2. Aukerman, Robert C. *Approaches to Reading Instruction.* New York: John Wiley and Sons, 1971.
3. Barker, George C. "Social Functions of Language in a Mexican American Community," *Acta Americana,* 1 (July–September 1947).
4. Campbell, R. N., and J. W. Lindfors. *Insights into English Structure.* Englewood Cliff, New Jersey: Prentice-Hall, 1969.
5. Cardenas, Daniel. *Applied Linguistics—Spanish.* Boston: D. C. Heath, 1961.
6. Critchlow, Donald E. *Dos Amigos Verbal Language Scales Manual.* San Rafael, California: Academic Therapy Publications, 1974.
7. Dechant, Emerald. *Improving the Teaching of Reading.* Englewood Cliffs, New Jersey: Prentice-Hall, 1964.
8. Forgione, José D. *La lectura y la escritura por el método global.* Buenos Aires: Editorial El Ateneo, 1965.
9. Green, Jerald R. *Spanish Phonology for Teachers: A Programed Introduction.* Philadelphia: Center for Curriculum Development, 1970.
10. Herbert, Charles H., and Antonio R. Sancho. *Spanish Reading Charts.* Austin, Texas: Dissemination Center for Bilingual-Bicultural Education, 1972.
11. Instituto Nacional de Pedagogía. *Guía didactica para la lectura-escritura.* Mexico: Editorial Grijalbo, S.A., 1968.
12. Kottmeyer, William. *Decoding and Meaning: A Modest Proposal.* New York: McGraw-Hill, 1974.
13. McDavid, Raven I. "Dialect Differences and Intergroup Tensions," *Studies in Linguistics,* 9 (1951), 27–33.
14. Maíllo, Adolfo. *Libro del maestro para la enseñanza activa del idioma.* Barcelona: Editorial Teide, 1965.
15. Martínez, Emiliano, et al. *Santillana Bilingual Series.* New York: Santillana, 1972.

16. Ramirez, Alfonso R., et al. *Region One Literacy Lessons; Sonidos, letras y palabras.* Edinburg, Texas: Melton Book, 1972.
17. Saporta, Sol. "Problems in Comparison of the Morphemic System of English and Spanish," *Hispania,* 39 (March 1956), 36–38.
18. Saville, Muriel, and Rudolph Troike. *A Handbook of Bilingual Education.* Washington: Teachers of English to Speakers of Other Languages, 1971.
19. Smith, Edgar A. "Devereaux Readability Index," *Journal of Educational Research,* 54 (April 1961), 289–303.
20. Stockwell, Robert P., J. Donald Bowen, and John W. Martin. *The Grammatical Structures of English and Spanish.* Chicago: University of Chicago Press, 1965.
21. Thonis, Eleanor W. *Aprendamos a Leer.* Cambridge, Massachusetts: Jacaranda Press, 1975.
22. Verdier, Rafael. *La enseñanza de la ortografía en la escuela primaria.* Madrid: Diana, Artes Gráficas, 1963.
23. Weiss, M. Jerry. "The Qualities of Reading Instruction," *Reading World,* 14 (December 1974), 88–100.

IRA PUBLICATIONS COMMITTEE 1975–1976 Richard A. Earle, McGill University, *Chairing*/Janet R. Binkley, IRA/Faye R. Branca, IRA/Joseph T. Brennan, Duquesne University/Jacqueline Chaparro, San Diego County Department of Education/Robert Dykstra, University of Minnesota/Roger Farr, Indiana University/Mary Feely, IRA/Lloyd W. Kline, IRA/Peter B. Messmore, Florida Atlantic University/Theodore A. Mork, Western Washington State College/Clifford D. Pennock, University of British Columbia/Robert B. Ruddell, University of California at Berkeley/Zelda Smith, Gables Academy, Miami/Ralph C. Staiger, IRA/M. Hope Underwood, University of Wisconsin at Whitewater/Susan Wasserman, California State University at Northridge/Sam Weintraub, State University of New York at Buffalo/Carol K. Winkley, DeKalb, Illinois.

| DATE DUE | | | |
|---|---|---|---|
| MAY 19 '87 | | | |
| NOV 0 4 1999 | | | |
| | | | |
| | | | |
| | | | |
| | | | |
| | | | |
| | | | |
| | | | |
| | | | |
| | | | |
| | | | |
| | | | |
| | | | |
| | | | |
| | | | |
| | | | |
| | | | |
| GAYLORD | | | PRINTED IN U.S.A. |